IVP PRAXIS
EQUIPPING LEADERS FOR MINISTRY

DO356470

God has called us to ministry. But it's not enough to have a vision for ministry if you don't have the practical skills for it. Nor is it enough to do the work of ministry if what you do is headed in the wrong direction. We need both vision *and* expertise for effective ministry. We need *praxis*.

Praxis puts theory into practice. It brings cutting-edge ministry expertise from visionary practitioners. You'll find sound biblical and theological foundations for ministry in the real world, with concrete examples for effective action and pastoral ministry. Praxis books are more than the "how to" – they're also the "why to." And because *being* is every bit as important as *doing*, Praxis attends to the inner life of the leader as well as the outer work of ministry. Feed your soul, and feed your ministry.

If you are called to ministry, you know you can't do it on your own. Let Praxis provide the companions you need to equip God's people for life in the kingdom.

www.ivpress.com/praxis

Ministry in the Digital Age

Strategies and Best Practices for a Post-Website World

David T. Bourgeois

An imprint of InterVarsity Press
Downers Grove, Illinois

InterVarsity Press
P.O. Box 1400, Downers Grove, IL 60515-1426
World Wide Web: www.ivpress.com
E-mail: email@ivpress.com

InterVarsity Press® is the book-publishing division of InterVarsity Christian Fellowship/USA®, a movement of students and faculty active on campus at hundreds of universities, colleges and schools of nursing in the United States of America, and a member movement of the International Fellowship of Evangelical Students. For information about local and regional activities, write Public Relations Dept., InterVarsity Christian Fellowship/USA, 6400 Schroeder Rd., P.O. Box 7895, Madison, WI 53707-7895, or visit the IVCF website at <www.intervarsity.org>.

All Scripture quotations, unless otherwise indicated, are taken from THE HOLY BIBLE, NEW INTERNATIONAL VERSION®, NIV® Copyright © 1973, 1978, 1984, 2011 by Biblica, Inc.™ Used by permission. All rights reserved worldwide.

While all stories in this book are true, some names and identifying information in this book have been changed to protect the privacy of the individuals involved.

Cover design: David Fassett

Interior design: Beth Hagenberg

ISBN 978-0-8308-5661-9

Printed in the United States of America ∞

Library of Congress Cataloging-in-Publication Data

A catalog record for this book is available from the Library of Congress.

P	18	17	16	15	14	13	12	11	10	9	8	7	6	5	4	3	2	1
Y	28	27	26	25	24	23	22	21	20	19	18	17	16	15	14	13

Contents

■ ■ ■

Introduction

Christianity is fundamentally a communication event.
It is God revealing God's self to the world.
And God uses a large variety of media
to accomplish that revelation.

Shane Hipps[1]

In March 2012, the nonprofit organization Invisible Children released a thirty-minute video to publicize a campaign aimed at bringing a war criminal to justice. Within the first twenty-four hours, the video had been viewed over one million times on YouTube; within the first month, it had been viewed over eighty-six million times.[2] This success did not just happen by chance. Invisible Children had spent months developing a community of followers and then developed a strategy to leverage that interest for the campaign.[3]

Many organizations are now trying to copy the approach taken by Invisible Children and use this strategy for their own efforts. But this may not necessarily be the right way to go about it, because each organization is unique. A strategy developed by one organization may not translate into success for another.

This book is about developing your own strategy for success using digital tools. Whether you are part of a large ministry looking for some fresh ideas, a small church just getting into this Internet thing or an individual who wants to understand how to contribute to God's kingdom, this book will guide you down the path to developing an effective digital strategy.

The Internet is the greatest communication tool ever invented by humans. It is the most rapidly adopted communication technology of all time, available to over two billion people at the time of this writing.[4] Social media sites such as Facebook and YouTube are growing at a fast pace, with Facebook garnering over one billion user accounts in seven years and YouTube now receiving eight hundred million unique users watching over four billion hours of video every month.[5]

If it is true, as Shane Hipps says, that Christianity is fundamentally a communication event, then it is imperative that Christians understand how to use the Internet well. This book was not written to convince you that the Internet or social media is important or that your ministry should use it. Since you have picked up this book, you already believe this to be true. I have written this book for one purpose: *to provide churches and ministries with the guidance they need to successfully embrace and use digital technologies as a means to fulfill their mission.*

Being successful online is not easy. Digital technologies are changing and evolving constantly. Websites that were once useful and efficient are now outdated (remember MySpace?). Even the logos and colors we use must keep up with the latest styles; what previously looked cutting edge may now convey the message that your ministry doesn't "get it" anymore.

And it isn't just the technologies that are changing; user expectations are as well. Just as television-viewers came to expect first color, then stereo sound, and now high-definition, the visitors to your website and Facebook page have also raised their expectations. Users today expect to be able to interact with your site. They expect video. They expect to be able to view your site on their mobile device. They don't want to have to work hard to find you: they expect you to come to them. I can sum it up this way: *they expect a relationship.*

Thinking Strategically

The single most important thing you can do for your ministry's use of the Internet and social media is to design, document and implement a digital strategy. It is not enough to rely on one person in your ministry to put up an attractive website or to give a volunteer the task of managing your Facebook page. You must be intentional.

A well-planned strategy will have several components, from initial planning to tool selection to implementation and follow-up. But even more than that, a good digital strategy must encompass the full range of activities necessary to be successful online. This means that your ministry must focus on more than just the technology; it must also focus on the *people* who are involved in the online ministry and the *processes* that must be put in place to ensure that all tasks are completed. All three of these components—technology, people and process—are equally important for a successful online ministry. I call this the *digital ministry framework*, and it is one of the core concepts in this book.

How does this play out? What value does a specific strategy for your digital ministry have? A well-thought-out digital strategy will enable you to answer some of the important questions about your ministry and will guide you through key decisions that you will have to make. Here are just a few of those questions and decisions.

Technology

- Should your ministry be on Facebook? Should you use a Facebook page or a Facebook group?

- How are people going to find your website? What steps have you taken to make this more likely?

- What search terms are people using to find you? Where do you show up in a web search of those terms?

- What does your website look like on a smartphone? Would an iPhone app be appropriate for your ministry? What about the iPad or other mobile devices?

People

- Who are you primarily targeting with your Internet presence? What percentage of that group uses the Internet daily? Or uses Facebook? Or has an iPhone?

- Who is responsible for your digital presence? Is it in that person's job description? Does she or he have the authority needed to be successful?

- What roles are appropriate for volunteers, and what should be assigned only to paid staff?

Process

- Who has to approve new content for the website or Facebook page?

- Do the appropriate people within your ministry have the ability to directly change the online information they are responsible for? Should they?

- What are the specific, measurable goals for your online ministry? What methods are you using to measure those goals? What will you do if you do not meet them?

- What is your process for making changes to parts of your digital ministry? When do you decide to shut something down?

A well-developed strategy can address these questions and decisions and many more. In this book, I will walk you through the steps necessary to develop the digital strategy that is right for your ministry. I will also introduce you to my research project on digital ministry best practices, which is based on this same framework. Using a combination of research and examples, the digital strategy framework will guide you through the creation of a plan that will allow you to be confident that your use of digital technologies is on the right track.

My prayer for you and your ministry is that you will be inspired and encouraged to take these specific steps for your digital ministry. Whether you are just beginning to use the Internet and social media for your ministry or you have been online for years, the concepts and recommendations outlined in this book will give you the opportunity to make full use of digital technologies.

1

What Hath God Wrought?

So we are at one of the great inflection points, I would argue,
in our history. I think this is going to be as big
as Gutenberg when it plays out.

Thomas Friedman[1]

When I was a little boy, I frequently wished that I could have lived during Bible times. Have you ever wished that you lived during the time that Christ walked the earth? Do you ever wish you could hear him speak and see his life? Or maybe you want to experience the time of Moses and the exodus from Israel? Or see the full splendor of God's blessing on Israel during the reign of Solomon? Many Christians would like to live in an era in which they could sense God moving. Well, fasten your seatbelts! It is my belief that we are living in one of those times right now: a time in which we will begin to see God working in a mighty way.

God's Story Is All Around Us

In Matthew 24, Jesus' disciples ask him to describe what it will be like when he returns. As part of his response, Jesus says to them, "And this gospel of the kingdom will be preached in the whole world as a testimony to all nations, and then the end will come" (Matthew 24:14).

If you're like me, you have read this passage many times before, trying to understand just how this will happen. Will we send missionaries to every single people group on earth? Will we translate the Bible into every language? Maybe. But I believe that God will be using digital technologies as the primary tool for accomplishing this.

This capability is just the next step in an evolution of communication technologies that has taken place since the time of Christ. In fact, Christians have frequently been at the forefront of utilizing these technologies as tools for fulfilling the Great Commission. To understand the role of these new and powerful technologies today, let us first take a look at how Christians have used technology in the past. We can then use this history to see how God is moving today.

The Roman roads. One of the very first technologies to be used for the cause of Christ was the road system implemented during the time of the Roman Empire. Though the Jews hated being under the rule of Rome, it was just this circumstance that allowed for the gospel to spread so quickly after the ascension of Christ in Acts 1.

> The possibilities of spreading the gospel afforded by this swift and safe method of travel were fully exploited by the early Christians, and both the New Testament and the literature of the second century simply take for granted journeys of enormous length which would scarcely have been possible after the fall of the Empire until modern times. . . . It is clear from the pages of the Acts that Christians made the maximum use of the Roman road system, and that it formed an unconscious directive to their evangelism. What a merchant could do for financial advantage, a Christian could do in the cause of the gospel.[2]

It is here, in those first few years of Christianity, that we see our brothers and sisters in Christ embracing the use of technology as a method for spreading the gospel.

The codex. During the time of Christ, the sacred Scriptures were written down in scrolls. But by the end of the first century, a new medium was coming into existence: the codex. A codex is much like today's book, with pages bound together and a cover surrounding the outside. The text was still handwritten, sometimes on both sides of the page. As you might imagine, a codex is much easier to transport than a scroll. It is also much easier to conceal, allowing a persecuted church to more easily distribute their Scriptures. While those in the early church did not invent the codex, they were quick to see its value and take advantage of this new technology.[3]

The printing press. In 1440, Johannes Gutenberg invented the first movable-type printing press. Before the invention of the printing press, copying written materials was a slow, tedious process. This ability to standardize the creation of printed materials revolutionized communications and had a huge impact on the world.

The impact of the printing press cannot be overstated: it brought about advancements in science, increased literacy rates and changed the power structure of information management. More importantly, it changed the way we viewed our world. After the invention of the printing press, there was an explosion of printed materials available to read. Because of this, it became imperative to be literate.

Christians were also among the first to immediately see the value in this technology. Martin Luther used it to transmit his Ninety-Five Theses; Gutenberg himself used it to print Bibles. And not only did he perfect the printing press; he also understood its implications for the furthering of God's kingdom. Gutenberg, in a preface to the Gutenberg Bible (1454), wrote, "God suffers in the multitude of souls whom His word can not reach. Religious truth is imprisoned in a small number of manuscript books, which confine instead of spread the public treasure. Let us break the seal which seals up holy things and give wings to Truth in order that she may win every soul that comes into the world by her word no longer written at great expense by hands easily palsied, but multiplied like the wind by an untiring machine."

The telegraph. On May 24, 1844, a new communication technology was introduced that had a transforming effect on the way the world communicated. The telegraph allowed, for the first time, information to be transmitted from one place to another in an instant. What used to take several days to communicate could now be done in just a few minutes. This new technology had a profound effect on our society over the following decades. It rewrote the rules of business, provided a new form of interpersonal relationships and brought a new optimism that the world could become a better place. Recognizing the importance of his new invention on that fateful day in 1884, inventor Samuel Morse sent the first message: "What hath God wrought?"[4]

While the application of the telegraph to reach the world for Christ was more limited than some of the previous technologies mentioned here, this was yet another step toward the fulfilling of the Great Commission. Again, as with Gutenberg, those living through this time of change saw God's hand working. In 1858, Charles F. Briggs and Augustus Maverick wrote the following in their book about the telegraph.

> For what is the end to be accomplished but the most spiritual ever possible? Not the modification or transportation of matter but the transmission of thought. To effect this an agent is employed so subtle in its nature that it may more properly be called a spiritual than a material force. The mighty power of electricity sleeping latent in all forms of matter in the earth, the air, the water; permeating every part and particle of the universe, carrying creation in its arms, it is yet invisible and too subtle to be analysed. . . . How potent a power then is the telegraphic destined to become in the civilization of the

world! This binds together by a vital cord all the nations of the earth. It is impossible that old prejudices and hostilities should longer exist, while such an instrument has been created for an exchange of thought between all the nations of the earth.[5]

Broadcast: Radio and television. At the turn of the twentieth century, we were yet again introduced to a new communications breakthrough. Unlike the telegraph (and its follow-up, the telephone), which had to be connected via a wire and only allowed point-to-point communication, radio allowed one person to reach many locations at the same time. This new "broadcast" technology allowed us to be in multiple places at once, reaching more people with the gospel of Christ than ever before.

Again, Christians were some of the first to see the power of this technology. Sixty of the first 709 radio licenses issued were issued to Christian organizations.[6] Many more paid for time on larger networked stations. Early pioneers included Aimee Semple McPherson, Charles Fuller, the Moody Bible Institute, and the Bible Institute of Los Angeles (now Biola University). Even today, the Far East Broadcasting Company spreads the gospel in 154 languages to people all over Southeast Asia using radio technology.[7]

Speaking of the value of radio for the cause of Christ, Aimee Semple McPherson, founder of the Foursquare Church, stated: "These are the days of invention! The days when the impossible has become possible! Days more favorable than any that ever have been known for the preaching of the blessed Gospel of our Lord and Saviour, Jesus Christ! Now, the crowning blessing, the most golden opportunity, the most miraculous conveyance for the message has come—The Radio!"[8]

Radio's big brother, television, continued this trend. Television began taking hold in the 1950s in the United States, and by 1971, it was reported that 47 percent of Americans listened to at least one religious broadcast (radio or TV) per week. Just as before, Christians began leading the way with these new technologies. In 1977, industry magazine *Broadcasting* singled out Pat Robertson's Christian Broadcasting Network (CBN) as a leader among all station operators, religious and secular, for its expertise in satellite communications.[9] Broadcast technologies have been very effective. According to Ben Armstrong in his book *The Electric Church*, more people became Christians between 1850 and 1950 than in all the previous years combined.[10]

That was then . . . As we have seen, Christians have been at the forefront of many of the previous revolutions in communication technologies, using these new tools to reach the world for Christ in new ways. What seemed impossible in Matthew 24:14 has become more and more possible to those who dream big for Christ.

But what about today? What about the part of the story we are in right now? We are no longer in the broadcast era. We are in the digital era.

The Digital Era

The term *digital* refers to the fact that today's computing devices, at their most basic level, can only speak in terms of ones and zeroes. This is true for any device that has a microprocessor chip inside of it: computers, mobile phones, digital televisions and even your new car. These digital technologies are revolutionizing the way we interact with each other, and it is through these digital technologies that we will continue to reach the world for Christ.

Of all the digital technologies that have come along in the past few years, the Internet has had the biggest impact. In fact, most of the digital devices developed in the past few years are really just different means for us to communicate over the Internet.

In the late 1960s, the Internet was developed as a digital-networking platform that enabled computers to communicate. But that definition is no longer enough. Now that the Internet can be accessed on a multitude of devices, anytime, anywhere, we have to expand this definition to go beyond computers.

So what is the Internet? Simply put, the Internet is a platform for enabling communications and applications over a digital network. That is not the official, technical definition, but it captures what the Internet has become today and it is the one we will be using in this book as we work to understand how to best utilize it for ministry.

You've got mail. Although it was originally designed to enable computer communications, the real power of the Internet began to emerge when it allowed person-to-person communication. The first sign that this was going to be the case was with the invention of electronic mail, or email. When this "simple program" was first released in 1971 by Ray Tomlinson, it took over the Internet (called ARPAnet in those days). The engineers and academics who put the ARPAnet together could not believe it! Email quickly became the most popular use of this new technology. It was the "killer app," driving the growth of the Internet beyond just scientific use to something that everybody wanted.

Over the next four decades, we have seen the same pattern hold true: Internet technologies that connect people together have driven the use of the Internet and associated technologies to new levels. From instant messaging to Skype to Facebook, this has continued to be the case. Technologies that allow people to connect with others drive new innovations and trends.

This powerful ability to connect people as never before should draw us, as followers of Christ, to the Internet. It is not about the latest gadget; it is about relationships. That is what makes these digital technologies so powerful for ministry. We need to understand that the Internet should first and foremost be about creating relationships: relationships between individuals, relationships between groups of people and relationships with God.

That everyone may hear. Our world is encircled with fiber optic cable. Fiber optic cable is the primary backbone of the Internet; it allows for digital communications at almost the speed of light. In a talk at the Massachusetts Institute of Technology (MIT) in 2005, Thomas Friedman explained how this came to be: "Netscape triggered the dot-com boom, and that triggered the dot-com bubble, and that triggered the accidental, ridiculous, absurd, outrageous, insane overinvestment of something close to a trillion dollars in fiber optic cable in five years. And that crazy, absurd, ridiculous investment of nearly a trillion dollars in fiber optic cable in five years accidentally made Beijing, Bangalore and Bethesda, where I live, next-door neighbors, without anyone, anywhere planning it to happen."[11]

According to Friedman, the fact that the world is now wired was just a happy "accident." I beg to differ. Just as I believe the Roman roads existed two thousand years ago to allow Christianity to quickly take root, I believe that God planned for this digital infrastructure at the beginning of the twenty-first century for his purposes as well. By combining the invention of the Internet with a free-market economic system that allowed for speculation in the late 1990s, I believe that God made the deployment of a worldwide communications infrastructure possible. Can we truly believe that God did not have a hand in that?

You've got the whole world in your hands. With the world wired for the Internet, what device will be most effective for communication? Not the computer. According to the highly respected technology research and consulting firm Gartner Group, by 2014 there will be almost as many mobile phone subscriptions as people on earth.

By 2013, mobile phones could easily surpass PCs as the way most people hop onto the web. Gartner's statistics show that the total number of PCs will reach 1.78 billion in three years, while the number of smartphones and Web-enabled phones will shoot past 1.82 billion units and continue to climb after that. This trend will force more Websites to revamp their pages to make them easier to surf on a mobile gadget. More than 3 billion people in the world will bank and shop online by 2014, thanks to advances in technology and growing Internet use among emerging markets, Gartner forecasts. Although cash won't be going away anytime soon, a base for electronic commerce will be firmly entrenched within the next four years. With 6.5 billion mobile connections expected by 2014, Gartner notes that not everyone with a mobile phone will conduct business online, but that all will have the ability to do so.[12]

To the ends of the earth. In Matthew 24, Jesus is speaking to his disciples about his second coming. Being human, as we all are, they are asking for a sign. "'Tell us,' they said, 'when will this happen, and what will be the sign of your coming and of the end of the age?'" (Matthew 24:3). In the next few verses, Jesus answers them, warning them of hardships to come. "And this gospel of the kingdom will be preached in the whole world as a testimony to all nations, and then the end will come" (Matthew 24:14). This is the story of which we are all a part. This is what is happening right now.

In 2004, former Silicon Valley executive Walt Wilson founded Global Media Outreach (GMO) because he, too, believed that we are part of this story. Since its founding, GMO has reached tens of millions with the message of Christ and has seen millions make a decision to follow him. Speaking of Matthew 24:14 and the Internet, Wilson said:

I believe that God has built this network to accomplish that very purpose within our lifetime. We are the first generation in all of human history to hold within our hands the technology to reach every man, woman, and child on the earth by 2020. We are being called to engage in the battle for human souls, all across the world. We are being given the tools to meet them in their time of need. The moment they step out of the darkness, we are there to meet them. . . . We have to get our people out of the pew and into the battle and this is the tool to do it.[13]

Ministry in the Digital Age is intended to prepare those who want to be a part of this story. The goal of this book is to help you understand how to think about and use these latest communication technologies as you work to reach the world for Jesus Christ.

2

Getting in the Stream

Forty-eight percent of 18- to 34-year-olds check Facebook
right when they wake up. . . . About 28 percent check
their Facebook on their smartphones
before getting out of bed.

2011 study from Online Schools[1]

■■■ ■

How can we get started using digital tools? How do we determine which tools to use? Many ministries think they know the answer: their website. Many hours and much expense are being put into developing exciting, robust websites that nobody is reading.

You see, we are now living in a *post-website* world. I don't know exactly when it happened, but sometime in the past few years, there has been a move away from the organizational website as the primary way that people interact with organizations. The massive popularity of social networking and the rise in mobile phone usage have changed the game. The key to understanding this is simple: the primary use of digital tools is now relational, not informational.

Take Your Message to the People

As you think about using digital tools for your ministry, your focus should be on how to develop relationships with your constituents. You need to understand them and know how they use digital tools. The question should change from "How do we make our website better?" to "How do we integrate into the digital habits of our audience?"

When I tell people that we are in a post-website world, many times I get a defensive or even angry response. Don't get me wrong: I am not saying that you don't need a website! A website is your "stake in the ground"; it is how people will find information about you if they are looking for it. But you should no longer think of it as your first, or even primary, means of interacting with the public.

So if they are not stopping by organizational websites, then what exactly are people doing online? The answer is simple: they are connecting with other people. This is being driven by the convergence of two technologies: social media and mobile technologies.

Table 2.1. Top 10 Sites on the Web

1	Google	google.com
2	Facebook	facebook.com
3	YouTube	youtube.com
4	Yahoo!	yahoo.com
5	Amazon.com	amazon.com
6	Wikipedia	wikipedia.org
7	eBay	ebay.com
8	Twitter	twitter.com
9	Craigslist.org	craigslist.org
10	Windows Live	live.com

Source: Alexa, the Web Information Company. http://www.alexa.com/topsites/countries/US

Let's take Facebook as an example. Not only has Facebook moved to the number two spot of the "most visited" list, but it has also moved to number one in the "time spent on site" list, with the average user spending over six hours per month on the site (as of August 2012)![2]

So what does this mean for a ministry's digital strategy? If you want to get your content in front of your audience, you must go where they are. Just as Christ went out of his way to find people in need and built relationships with them, so your ministry must determine where your audience is and go to them to build a relationship through your online presence.

If You Build It, They Will *Not* Come

Many will look at these data and this shift toward more interactive and social online activity and draw the conclusion that their ministry should build its own social network or other interactive site. *This is absolutely the wrong conclusion!* If you knew that your potential audience went to Starbucks every day and you wanted to engage with them, would you first build your own coffeehouse down the street and then tell them, "Come to my shop; I'll be waiting"? No. Your best strategy would be to go to Starbucks yourself and interact with them there. There are very few situations in which creating your own environment for interacting with your audience makes sense.

We need to go where the people are. The first step is to find out just where they are! Do your research and find out where the people you want to reach are going, and then go there yourself. This will be a key step in developing your digital strategy. We will discuss methods for doing this kind of research later in this book.

Just as email was the driving force behind the initial expansion of the Internet, social media are now driving more and more people online for longer periods of time. It is these new social media habits that you want to become a part of. To do this, you must insert your ministries into the *streams* of information that wash over these users every day. To have the maximum reach possible, we must understand the streams that our potential audience wades through on a daily basis and become part of them.

Types of Streams

What do I mean by *streams*? Simply put, a stream is the flow of digital content that our potential audience puts in front of themselves every day. Anyone who uses a digital device has these streams. They are the daily habits that we all have in the use of our devices. Every time we sit down in front of a screen, we are turning on the digital tap and drinking from it. Streams can be found in many places online.

- *Facebook*. Right now, Facebook is the number one place people spend their time online. People are constantly viewing status updates and posting notes. Depending on your target audience, this may be the best way to get into people's streams.

- *Text messages*. Depending upon your generation, this may be the stream you drink from most often. How can you leverage text messaging for your ministry?

- *Email*. Many people still use email as their primary online communication and relationship tool. The demographic for the primary use of email skews a little bit older, but this may be where your ministry needs to be.

- *Twitter*. Twitter use is growing and is accessible in many different ways. Though not necessarily used by a large percentage of people, Twitter tends to be used by those who are highly influential and digitally savvy.

- *Search results*. If people are looking for you, can they find you? While we may be in a post-website world, you need to be ready if someone does want to find out more about you! Search engine results are still one of the most important ways to get your content in front of people. But don't be surprised if your Facebook page or Twitter feed get higher rankings than your website!

- *Wikipedia.* Many people go to Wikipedia first when trying to find information, and Wikipedia results almost always show up in the first page of search results. Do some research to see if there are any options for your ministry in Wikipedia.[3]

- *News reader.* The more tech-savvy people out there, and those who do a lot of reading on the web, probably use an RSS (Rich Site Summary) reader to aggregate content into one place. An RSS reader allows the user to find all of their news stories and blog posts in one place. Be sure that your content is compatible with an RSS reader.

This idea—placing your organization where people are located—is nothing new. Marketers have been thinking in these terms for decades. Billboards, television and radio ads, door-to-door salespeople, telemarketers, and multi-level marketing companies are all evidence of this. Our potential "customers" will not come to us or engage with us unless we go to them first. Of course, many of these methods have an extremely negative connotation for Christians; we may not want our ministry to be identified with the tactics of telemarketing or even advertising. So do we forget the idea of streams and just build a great website, hoping that people will visit it? No.

Building Digital Relationships

As I stated earlier, the key to this post-website world is relationships. The main focus of our digital communications and interactions should be *building relationships*. Your digital ministry will not be viewed as a marketing campaign if it is truly intended to build relationships. To do this, you need a carefully crafted strategy that is research-based and encompasses a variety of methods. Below are some tips for using this idea of streams for building relationships.

- *Identify each stream and its potential role in your overall digital strategy.* The number of content items you place into a stream should be enough to get noticed but not so much that it is considered spam. Remember: users have control over their own stream. They can unsubscribe from your mailing list, block your Facebook posts and stop following you on Twitter.

- *Think about how you will initiate a new relationship.* Will you post ads asking people to "like" or "follow" you? Will you look for recommendations through friends?

- *If you choose to have multiple streams (and you probably should), find tools that allow you to manage them from one place.* For example, if you post to Facebook and Twitter, you can link them together so that you only need to do one update. Many third-party tools can help with this.

- *If email is one of your streams, consider using a tool that will help you manage your email campaigns.* Such a tool will allow you to manage your distribution lists and keep track of who actually reads the emails you are sending.

- *Don't offend.* If it is not appropriate for your content to be delivered through one of these methods, then don't! Remember that each stream has unique pros and cons (we will examine this in more detail in chapter 3). Some are more public than others. Examine each thoroughly.

- *Decide who is going to manage the streams.* Don't think this aspect of your organization will run itself! Someone on staff should have this in their job description. For example, if you decide to create a Facebook presence for your ministry that allows people to write posts to your page, who is going to monitor them for inappropriate content? Who will respond when a question is posted?

SOCIAL MEDIA MANAGEMENT TOOLS

As you work to determine what digital streams you want to generate for your ministry, you will also want to consider exactly how you will manage those streams. There are many tools available that will greatly simplify the management of social media and email campaigns.

Hootsuite will help you manage all your social media accounts, allowing you to post to Facebook, Twitter and other social networks from one place. Hootsuite will also allow you to schedule your posts so that they will post at some point in the future. This allows you to create a regular set of posts each week for your ministry. Besides Hootsuite, you may want to take a look at similar tools such as Tweetdeck or Seesmic.

For email campaigns, take a look at a tool such as Constant Contact. For a very reasonable monthly fee, Constant Contact will manage your mailing lists, provide you with templates for your emails and give you statistics on who is reading your messages and what links they are clicking on. Constant Contact also integrates with social media well, allowing you to combine your email streams with your social media streams. Besides Constant Contact, you may want to check out MailChimp or GetResponse.

The Move to Mobile

In addition to living in a post-website world, we are also in a *post-PC* world. Simply put, the computer as we have come to know it will no longer be the primary way in which people will interact with your digital content. We are moving to a wireless, mobile environment very quickly. Of course, the personal computer will continue to be used, but it will not be the primary device through which users will interact with your content.

Speaking at an Internet conference in March 2010, Google's European director of online sales said simply: "In three years' time, desktops will be irrelevant."[4] The move to wireless mobile devices with intuitive interfaces will be the norm, not the exception. Devices such as smartphones and tablet computers will become the dominant way people get online. And as you read in the first chapter, the Gartner Group reports that by 2014, there will be 6.5 billion mobile connections to the Internet—virtually one mobile device for every person in the world.[5]

As with the move to social media, the statistics back up this move to mobile. Venture capitalist Mary Meeker, in her highly anticipated 2011 research report, notes that the adoption of "mobile Internet" is the fastest technology adoption in our history. Simply put, we are accessing the Internet on our mobile devices at a faster rate than we adopted radio, television or PC-based Internet.[6]

So what does this mean for ministry? It means that your online strategy should assume that your audience will want to access your content on mobile devices. This access can be provided in various ways, including a mobile version of your website and/or a mobile app. You should begin thinking *now* about how your ministry's online content will appear when accessed this way. But how do you do this?

Not Just a Smaller Version of Your Website

In the book *Mobile Persuasion,* the authors make clear that designing for mobile is *much more* than just making a website fit inside a smaller screen. They claim that "the mobile-human relationship is one of the most personal, intensive, and lasting of all relationships."[7] If your goal is to develop a relationship with your online users, then what better way to do so than through their mobile device?

The authors of *Mobile Persuasion* also warn that "developing a mobile 'experience' is fundamentally different from a web experience. The experience is not only 'smaller,' but should also be 'smarter.'" They go on to conclude that "being mobile is much less about technology, and much more about culture, connectedness, and fundamental human needs."[8]

MOBILE APP OR MOBILE WEBSITE?

As you consider making your digital presence compatible with mobile devices, you will be confronted with the decision of just how to do so. Your first thought might be to quickly develop a mobile app that users can download to their phones to obtain information about your ministry. But this is probably not the best first choice for going mobile.

A mobile app is an expensive proposition, and it will only run on one type of mobile device at a time. For example, if you create an iPhone app, people with Android phones are out of luck. Each app takes several thousand dollars to create, so this may not be the best use of your funds.

Instead, I recommend the first step that any ministry take is to simply ensure that their existing website works well on a mobile device. A mobile website works on all mobile devices and costs about the same as creating an app (see chart on next page). This may require taking some time thinking through how a mobile version of your website should look and spending some money on designing it. You may want to simplify what people find there. For example, many people using a mobile device to find your site may be looking for an address to plug in to their GPS, so you may want to make that easily available on the mobile version of your site.

Once you have your website working well on mobile, then it is time to consider if you also need an app. A mobile app can provide a very engaging experience for your users and can be an improvement over a mobile website. Table 2.2 offers several comparisons between apps and websites.[9]

Table 2.2. Website and App Comparisons

Channel	Cost to Build	Percentage of Mobile Phones Reached	Number of People Per $
Mobile Website	$30,000	51%	7,800
Mobile App (iPhone)	$30,000	16%	1,254
Mobile App (all platforms)	$90,000	48%	1,266

Developing for the mobile environment, at least in 2013, is not a simple task. But just as developing for the computer-based browser has become so much easier in the past few years, I believe that developing for mobile devices will also become much easier. One simple solution for developing for mobile would be to simply become part of a site that already has a mobile interface. For example: YouTube, Facebook and Twitter already work well on mobile devices, so creating a presence on one or more of these sites will automatically put your organization on mobile devices.

Start Wading In Now

It is crucial that your ministry begins to focus on being both social and mobile. You will need to understand the streams of information that your organization's potential audience values, and you will need to determine the best way to build an online relationship with them. These will be key parts of your digital strategy, as we will see in the upcoming chapter.

3

Creating Change

An organization becomes irrelevant when the change
outside the organization exceeds the change
inside the organization.

Walt Wilson[1]

In 2010 I had the opportunity to meet and interview Walt Wilson, the founder of Global Media Outreach. When I asked him about how the organization got started, he told me that he simply asked himself the question: "If missions, evangelism, discipleship and church buildings did not already exist, how would we do it (bring people to Christ)?" Starting with the idea that God's Word is so powerful that it can stand alone to convict those who are seeking God, Wilson stepped completely out of the traditional model for missions and created a brand new model. Wilson had watched people who were presented with the gospel face-to-face fall on their knees through the working of the Holy Spirit. So he began to ask, "Why can't we do the same thing over the Internet?" As he said to me, the work of Global Media Outreach is just "straight talk on the Internet. It's not rocket science; we just present the four spiritual laws."[2] And thus began the journey of Global Media Outreach. In just over seven years, the organization has seen more than fifty million people make decisions for Christ through its ministry, and thousands more are being discipled every day.

Keep the Change?

Change is occurring at a rapid pace outside the church, and we risk becoming irrelevant if we cannot keep up. We've all heard the staggering numbers regarding the Internet: the pace at which the Internet is changing is phenomenal. Just over ten years ago, in the year 2000, only 124 million people in the United States had access to the Internet (44 percent of the total population); 360 million people worldwide had access (just 6 percent of the total population). Today, 245 million people in the United States have access to the Internet (78 percent of the population) and 2.3 billion worldwide do (33 percent). So while the trends in the U.S. must flatten out, worldwide growth continues unabated.[3]

And how is the Internet being used? According to the Pew Internet & American Life Project, we are using it for just about everything! From online banking to email to getting news to watching videos, we are doing more and more online. See tables 3.1 and 3.2 for more information on who is using the Internet and how.[4]

Table 3.1. Demographics of Internet Users

	% who use the Internet
Total adults	78
Men	78
Women	78
Race/ethnicity	
White, Non-Hispanic	79
Black, Non-Hispanic	67
Hispanic (English- and Spanish-speaking)	78

	% who use the Internet
Age	
18-29	95
30-49	87
50-64	74
65+	42
Household income	
Less than $30,000/yr	63
$30,000-$49,999	85
$50,000-$74,999	89
$75,000+	96
Educational attainment	
Less than High School	42
High School	69
Some College	89
College+	94
Community type	
Urban	79
Suburban	80
Rural	72

Table 3.2. Online Activities

	% of adult Internet users in the U.S. who do this online	Survey month/day/year
Use a search engine to find information	91	2/1/2012
Send or read email	91	8/1/2011
Look for information on a hobby or interest	84	8/1/2011
Search for map or driving directions	84	8/1/2011
Check the weather	81	5/1/2010

	% of adult Internet users in the U.S. who do this online	Survey month/day/year
Look for health/medical information	80	9/1/2011
Look for information online about a service or product you are thinking of buying*	78	9/1/2010
Get news	76	5/1/2011
Go online just for fun or to pass the time	74	8/1/2011
Buy a product	71	5/1/2011
Watch a video on a video-sharing site like YouTube or Vimeo	71	5/1/2011
Search for information about someone you know or might meet*	69	9/1/2009
Look for "how-to," "do-it-yourself" or repair information	68	8/1/2011
Visit local, state or federal government website*	67	5/1/2011
Use a social networking site like Facebook, LinkedIn or Google Plus*	66	2/1/2012
Buy or make a reservation for travel	65	5/1/2011
Do any banking online	61	5/1/2011
Look online for news or information about politics	61	8/1/2011
Look online for information about a job*	56	5/1/2011
Look for information on Wikipedia	53	5/1/2011
Use online classified ads or sites like Craigslist	53	5/1/2011
Get news or information about sports*	52	1/1/2010

	% of adult Internet users in the U.S. who do this online	Survey month/day/year
Take a virtual tour of a location online	52	8/1/2011
Do any type of research for your job	51	3/1/2007
Upload photos to a website so you can share them with others online	46	11/1/2011
Send instant messages	46	12/1/2010
Pay to access or download digital content online*	43	8/1/2008
Look for information about a place to live*	39	8/1/2006
Download music files to your computer	37	12/1/2007
Get financial information online, such as stock quotes or mortgage interest rates	37	5/1/2010
Rate a product, service or person using an online rating system	37	5/1/2011
Play online games*	36	9/1/2010
Categorize or tag online content like a photo, news story or blog post	33	12/1/2008
Read someone else's online journal or blog*	32	5/1/2010
Look for religious/spiritual information	32	9/1/2010
Post a comment or review online about a product you bought or a service you received	32	9/1/2009
Post comments to an online news group, website, blog or photo site	32	9/1/2010
Share something online that you created yourself	30	9/1/2010

	% of adult Internet users in the U.S. who do this online	Survey month/day/year
Research your family's history or genealogy online*	27	9/1/2009
Download video files to your computer	27	12/1/2007
Participate in an online auction	26	9/1/2010
Make a donation to a charity online	25	5/1/2011
Make a phone call online, using a service such as Skype or Vonage	25	8/1/2011
Participate in an online discussion, a LISTSERV or other online group forum that helps people with personal issues or health problems*	22	12/1/2006
Download a podcast so you can listen to it or view it later*	21	9/1/2010
View live images online of a remote location or person, using a webcam	17	9/1/2009
Create or work on webpages or blogs for others, including friends, groups you belong to or work	15	9/1/2009
Take material you find online— like songs, text or images—and remix it into your own artistic creation	15	5/1/2008
Download or share files using peer-to-peer file-sharing networks, sut as BitTorrent or LimeWire	15	8/1/2006
Sell something online	15	9/1/2009
Use Twitter	15	2/1/2012
Create or work on your own webpage	14	1/1/2010
Create or work on your own online journal or blog*	14	5/1/2011

	% of adult Internet users in the U.S. who do this online	Survey month/day/year
Buy or sell stocks, bonds or mutual funds	11	9/1/2009
Use an online dating website*	8	9/1/2009
Visit virtual worlds such as Second Life	4	9/1/2009

*Item wording has changed slightly over time

As we discussed in the last chapter, another major change in the way we communicate is through the explosion in mobile phone growth. As of 2011, the number of mobile phone subscriptions in the United States hit 324 million, which is more than the population. Worldwide, there are now 4.6 billion mobile phones, representing a staggering 61 percent of the population. And while some people may have more than one mobile phone, this still means that over half the world's population now has a mobile phone. As referenced in chapter 1, the Gartner Group expects over six billion mobile phone users by the year 2014. That's virtually the entire world!

So how do we respond? As Walt Wilson and Global Media Outreach did, we need to look at these changes and respond with courage. But how do we go about changing? Is there a Christian response to change?

A Theology of Change

In *Church Next: Using the Internet to Maximize Your Ministry*, Aubrey and Michael Malphurs present the concept of a "theology of change."[5] Although the book is focused on how churches can change, the concepts are applicable for all ministries. The Malphurses point out that Christian organizations, and specifically churches, often view change as a bad thing. This negative view of change has led to resistance to it, which I have seen in many different organizations. Trying to bring change is threatening. It makes people uncomfortable, because we are asking them to get out of their comfort zones. Many times, when change is then forced on a ministry, it ends up going badly, reinforcing the notion that change is bad. But change is not always bad; change that is managed properly can have a positive effect and lead to a more effective organization. And this is important, because organizations that cannot change often simply die or become irrelevant.

Many churches and ministries have been reluctant to change because they are concerned about moving away from what has made them successful in the past. They have been doing something the same way for so long that they consider it the "right way" and do not want to change. Many are concerned that change could lead to heresy.

An interesting point that the Malphurses raise in their book is the question: "Is change biblical?" They explore this question further: "Of all the reasons for a church to be cautious about change, the risk of heresy is the most compelling. Church decline, the increase in the number of unchurched, and the growth of cults and nonreligious groups doesn't mean that the church should change if that would mean abandoning the faith. Some people argue that it will lead to that result, pointing to what has happened to the faith of the mainline churches. If this is the case, as some people fear, then change is out of the question."[6]

Yet we know we must change. How can we change without compromising our biblical principles? How do we do it without changing who we are as a ministry? The Malphurses' "theology of change" consists of three underlying components: *function, form and freedom*. Understanding the interrelationship between these three components will give you the tools you need to work through change in your ministry.

Function. The first of the three components of a theology of change is *function*. According to the Malphurses, functions are the "timeless, unchanging, nonnegotiable precepts based in scripture" that represent the core of your organization.[7] Identifying your ministry's functions, then, is the first step toward change.

How do you identify your ministry's functions? For most organizations, a starting point for identifying the functions is the mission statement. A mission statement is a sentence that encompasses the core of what your organization is about. A well-written mission statement will make it easy to understand what your ministry does and also will help you determine what it does not do.

Understanding your function is a real key to success with the digital part of your ministry as well. During my 2007-2008 research project on Internet best practices (available as appendix B), I interviewed the founder of a very successful online ministry. I asked him the question, "What one factor, more than any other, has led to your success?" He was quick to answer that for his organization, the critical factor was an understanding of their mission. He went on to tell me that an astounding 80 percent of their ideas for new functionality on their ministry's website are shot down because they don't match the mission!

As you develop your ministry's digital strategy, it will be very important to have a clear mission for your organization, one that is understood well by everyone involved in creating your digital strategy. But how is this done?

For churches (and some other ministries), functions can be identified by going directly to Scripture. For example, many churches will base their functions on the early church as described in Acts 2, with functions such as teaching, fellowship, communion and prayer. These are nonnegotiable, unchanging functions of the church.

If your organization does not have a basis for identifying its functions, then this is really your first step in working through change. It goes beyond the scope of this book to walk you through the creation of a mission statement, but many great resources exist to help you. A good one for churches is *Advanced Strategic Planning* by Aubrey Malphurs. For other ministries, you may want to check out *Managing the Nonprofit Organization: Principles and Practices* by Peter Drucker.[8]

When identifying the functions of your ministry, be sure you are describing them by *what* you do, not *how* you do them. For example, it would be incorrect for a church to identify one of its functions as "sermons on Sunday morning." Sermons are not a function; they are a form (which we will discuss next). A better way to identify this function would be "teaching" or "inspiring the congregation." Remember: a function is *what* your organization does, not *how* you accomplish it.

Form. The second component of change is *form*. According to the Malphurses, forms are the "temporal, changing, negotiable practices, based on an organization's culture and methods, that we are free to choose in order to accomplish our functions."[9] Functions are *what* an organization does, and forms are *how* it gets done.

Forms are not timeless; they are context-sensitive. One example of this is an experience I had just this past summer. In the past, in order to sign up my children for summer camp, I had to sit down and fill out multiple pages of forms. Now I simply log on to the camp's website, identify my children from their records, and update any information that has changed. The *function* of camp registration has stayed the same, but the *form* has changed.

Another example of this is the function of worship for a church. All churches perform the function of the worship of God; but how that function is carried out can be quite different for each church. Sometimes, even at the same church, the form worship takes may be quite different now than it was twenty years ago! From traditional hymns to chanting to upbeat music, worship has changed. The key point here is this: the *function* of worship is still being carried out, but the *form* has changed.

Forms are negotiable as well. This means that when a function is identified, it can take several possible forms. For example, a mission organization's function of communicating needs with supporters could take the form of a postal letter, a phone call, an email or a blog. In fact, it could take on more than one of these. The organization must endeavor to understand the best way to carry out this function.

This brings us to an important point about forms: in order to select a culturally relevant form that is appropriate to carry out an organization's function, an organization must know what forms are available. To do this requires becoming a *cultural observer*. The Malphurses put it this way: "To think and act strategically, churches must be cultural observers who survey the landscape in search of effective ways that God is using to work through churches in America and around the world to accomplish its biblically mandated functions."[10]

Being a cultural observer can be more difficult than it sounds. Frankly, it is impossible to have knowledge about every possible form that a function could take. As digital technologies change so quickly, there is no way for an organization to constantly be aware of all of the newest innovations and technologies. So how do we go about it?

- *Attend conferences*. Many conferences have at least one session or track devoted to the use of digital technologies.

- *Look at the websites of other ministries*. Find those ministries that you respect and take the time to see how they are engaging their audience with digital tools.

- *Scan books or periodicals devoted to your field of ministry*. Many different magazines and books are devoted to the topic of churches' and ministries' use of technology.

- *Read blogs devoted to ministry and technology*. Many ministry leaders write regularly about the use of technology and the Internet in ministry.

- *Talk with volunteers within your ministry who are familiar with the latest in technologies.* Find out who in your constituency or congregation is a leader, thinker or cutting-edge user in this area, and take them to lunch!

- *If you can afford it, bring in a consultant to review current technologies with you.* This may not be an option for all ministries or churches, but many organizations will work with churches and ministries to help them understand the best forms available.

Each function you identify may be able to take several different forms. Are we free to choose any form we want? Are there

BEING A CULTURAL OBSERVER

There are so many good resources that it is difficult to mention only a few here. But I also think that it is important to give everyone a starting point. Below are a few resources that will help you and your ministry be good cultural observers when it comes to the use of digital tools for ministry.

- Mashable (mashable.com). News and reviews on everything related to social media.
- Church Mag (churchm.ag). Opinions and reviews on the use of digital tools by churches and ministries.
- Internet Evangelism Day (internetevangelismday.com). A treasure trove of ideas and resources for using digital tools for the cause of Christ.
- Church Marketing Sucks (churchmarketingsucks.com). Good resource for discussing the use of digital tools for marketing and communications from a ministry perspective.

- Biola Digital Ministry Conference (cwc.biola.edu). Annual conference covering the latest in digital strategy and technology for ministry. See videos from this conference posted on YouTube at bit.ly/bioladigital.
- Christian Leadership Alliance Annual Conference—Ministry Internet Technology Summit (christian leadershipalliance.org). Hear from leaders in the field discussing the best ways to leverage these tools for your ministry.

any limits? This is where the third component of the Malphurses' theology of change can be applied.

Freedom. The third component of change is *freedom*. We are free to select any form we want, but there are limits on this freedom. First of all, the freedom only applies to our selection of forms, not to our functions. We must wisely select the most effective forms to carry out our function. In other words, although many forms may be possible to carry out our functions, not all of them are appropriate. So how do we choose? What are the limitations or guidelines?

Another way of addressing this issue is to remember that just because we *can* do something does not mean we *should* do something. For example, if your ministry offers marriage counseling, you could consider offering online counseling via video chat (such as Skype). This is surely technologically possible! But is it the best choice? I would suggest that, under almost all circumstances, offering a marriage counseling session in which the counselor and participants are not physically together does not provide the best form for that particular function.

The Malphurses also give the restriction that "the forms we choose must help us to accomplish our biblical functions."[11] It may be tempting to select a form because it is the latest trend or because everyone else is doing it. But a real analysis may show that this form does not really help us perform our function well. For example, it seems that many ministries are creating Twitter accounts because, well, everyone else has one. And while sending tweets may technically perform a function, such as "communicating with our constituents," is it really the best way to do it?

Consider the example of a pregnancy crisis center that has as one of its functions a counseling service to those who have an unexpected pregnancy. One of the forms this could take is offering email communication on the website. This form does accomplish the function. Further analysis, however, may find that email is a limiting form of communication that does not effectively lead to another possible function of the organization: developing a personal relationship with clients. On the other hand, the anonymity of email may make it a better choice for this sort of ministry. So while we are free to choose email communication, we must truly understand the function we are attempting to accomplish before we can determine the proper choice.

In addition to the limitations discussed above, I would add two more. First, when selecting forms for our ministry, we should be mindful of how we are using God's resources. When given a choice between different forms, we should consider how we are using the time, money and people that God has given our ministry. While it is important that we always present ourselves in the most excellent way, if we do not have the money to purchase a specific technology tool, we should not select it. For some ministries, the cost may not be the issue so much as the ability and time of someone to support it. Do not select a technology that will take you away from the core of your ministry.

The second limitation on our freedom to select a form that I would add is this: we should consider how our selection of a particular form will influence how those we are trying to serve perceive our organization and its mission. This is an important point, and one that we look at in the next section.

The Medium Is the Message

When determining which technologies to use and which functions of the ministry should be part of a digital strategy, we cannot forget the words of Marshall McLuhan: "the medium is the message." McLuhan coined this famous phrase in 1964, and it has been widely hailed as an insightful look into the power of media in our society. I don't know about you, but when I first began studying McLuhan, I did not fully understand exactly what "the medium is the message" meant. And I sure as heck did not see any relationship between it and ministry!

Then, in 2008, I read Shane Hipps's book *The Hidden Power of Electronic Culture*, and that all changed. Hipps's book, combined with more research and discussion on my part, led me to the conclusion that, indeed, the media we use to communicate our message can have a profound impact on our effectiveness and on how our audience perceives us. This concept must be a part of our discussion of a theology of change, because it is imperative that we understand the impact of the forms we choose to carry out our functions.

In his book, Hipps suggests that the church has often viewed technologies such as radio, TV and now the Internet as "just more tools" and believed that, as long as the message stays the same, then the medium used to transmit it does not matter. This line of thinking has led many ministries and churches to embrace all technologies instead of considering how the use of the technologies themselves sends a message. Hipps does not say that technology is bad, only that we need to be informed about how the use of a technology can change our message.

The conventional wisdom is that the choice of medium does not matter; technology is just a tool, after all. But this, according to McLuhan, is simply not true. Instead, he says, "Our conventional response to all media, namely that it is how they are used that counts, is the numb stance of the technological idiot. For the 'content' of a medium is like the juicy piece of meat carried by the burglar to distract the watchdog of the mind."[12] These are strong words, but strong words are needed. The use of a medium sends a message. And we must understand what that message is.

One recurring example that Hipps uses is the impact that print has had on the development of the Christian faith. Hipps puts it this way: "Paul was a highly literate person, and his letters reflect the kind of abstract if/then reasoning characteristic of a literate mind. This sits in contrast to the gospels, which are characterized by concrete storytelling rooted in the oral tradition. Prior to printing, medieval culture accessed Scripture largely through stained glass windows, which were well-suited to present the life of Jesus but were hard-pressed to articulate the dense theological reasoning of Paul's letters. The printing press not only provided an appropriate medium for Paul's message, but it also helped modern culture develop the reasoning skills necessary to comprehend his message."[13] Hipps goes on to discuss the impact, both good and bad, this has had on Christian culture and understanding.

So the use of any particular medium has an impact on the message we are trying to convey. What about digital tools such as the Internet or mobile phones: can these change our message? Yes. When specifically asked about how the Internet might change the message, Hipps suggested that the Internet is a medium that is used as a transport for a variety of other media, which implies that it can have a *huge* impact.[14]

For example, when we post a blog entry, expert opinion says we must keep the length short; if it is too long, no one will bother to read it. To work under this condition, many authors try to create a "quick hit" post about something that really requires more depth. And what about using video to stream a church service? Won't this lead many to view the service as they do television: just sit back and do the couch potato? This leads to a very different experience than attending a worship service in person.

As we work to understand the best way to use the Internet and social media for ministry, the question we should be asking is not, "*Does* the use of digital tools change the message of our ministry?" No. The question we should ask instead is, "*How* does the message change when it is communicated via these digital tools?"

So am I saying that ministries should abandon the Internet because it may lead to a changing of their message? No. But I do think it is very important for those of us who want to minister online to have an understanding of how the Internet changes our ministry's message and to use this knowledge to help us make decisions about how to use it.

Be Courageous

According to Walt Wilson, change occurs for two reasons: courage or crisis.[15] We should have the courage to change before we are in crisis mode and *must* change. By identifying your ministry's functions and then carefully choosing the appropriate forms for carrying them out, your ministry can begin to craft a strategy that will lead to successful use of the Internet.

4

The Digital Ministry Framework

The best way to predict your future is to create it.

Peter F. Drucker

In the first three chapters of this book, we saw how digital technologies have had a tremendous impact on our culture and the way we communicate, and we have seen the need for change. This sets the stage for the development of your digital ministry strategy.

When beginning to develop a strategy for your ministry's use of digital tools, you may naturally think about technology first. But this is backwards! If your ministry truly wants to develop a strategy for the use of digital tools, then technology is not the first or even primary concern. To put it bluntly: *technology is not the hard part.*

If technology is not the hard part, then what is? When I teach classes in the management of information systems, on the first day I usually offer the students a definition of an information system. An information system, I tell them, is made up of three basic components: technology, people and process. All three are equally important to understand; one is no more important than the others.

As I have been studying digital ministry over the past few years, I have become more and more convinced that these same three components are the underpinnings of any successful use of digital tools. Unfortunately, many organizations looking to start a digital ministry immediately focus on the technology and completely ignore the more difficult decisions surrounding the people involved and the processes undertaken to implement and maintain the ministry. I developed the *digital ministry framework* (see figure 4.1) to embody these three components and to provide a structure around which a ministry can develop a digital presence. Each component of the framework is composed of several different elements, all of which are crucial to successful implementation.

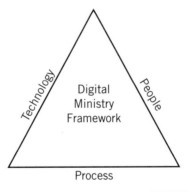

Figure 4.1. Digital ministry framework

In 2007 and 2008, I conducted a research project that looked to determine the best practices for those doing ministry online. More than three hundred ministries and churches took part in the research, which consisted of an online survey and follow-up interviews. Using the digital ministry framework as a backdrop, I was able to look at what successful ministries had in common in the areas of technology, people and process. Of those ministries who participated in the survey, only 36 percent reported their online ministry as "successful."[1] My report further analyzed the results to determine what these 36 percent had in common and reported these as the best practices. You can find the full research report as appendix B.

In this chapter, we will review each of the components—technology, people and process—and will spend time digging into what each term means. We will then see how each of these plays a role in the success of a digital ministry and is an important part of any digital strategy. Let's begin with technology.

Technology

As I mentioned earlier, technology is the component of the framework on which most ministries focus, many times to the exclusion of all else. For some, this is because that is what they know how to do. They are the "ministry technology nerds," who are constantly pushing the boundaries of technology and want to see their ministries do the same. For others, technology is difficult and scary, and therefore they think it will require the most effort and attention. In reality, *for most ministries, spending less time on technology and more on people and process will bring a better chance of success.*

The technology component of digital ministry includes not just website software but also decisions surrounding what other digital tools should be integrated into the ministry. Should you create YouTube videos? Should you prioritize the use of mobile devices? What about a mobile app? How will people find you on search engines? What statistics should you collect about how people use your website? These decisions (and many others) generally require someone with experience in digital technologies and how they can be used for ministry. Below are some good technology questions to ask when planning your digital ministry.

What functions are required for the ministry to succeed? When putting together a digital strategy, ministries often start by selecting the software or other digital technology they will use before even attempting to understand what they need it to do. For example, someone in the ministry will say, "We need to have a YouTube channel!" or "We need an app!" and then ask someone to build it. This is completely backwards. First you must understand the functions that you would like to accomplish in order to meet the goals of your ministry. Only then should you determine which digital tool will best meet those needs.

Should we build something ourselves or use an existing application? A previous chapter touched on this question, but I will reiterate it here: creating something brand new, such as a new website or social network, sometimes does not make sense. After you have understood the goals of your digital ministry and developed a set of functions that it should have, then you can take a look around to determine if there is an existing tool that would make the most sense. According to my best-practices research, those ministries that built their own websites were successful only 36 percent of the time, while those that purchased their technology solution reported success 59 percent of the time.

For example, if your ministry is looking for a way to communicate announcements and events to its supporters, it may make more sense to create a Facebook page and use its social networking and events features to accomplish these tasks rather than to add a blog to your existing webpage or purchase an email marketing program. On the other hand, if you have a requirement that really cannot be accomplished through an existing application, then building it or purchasing it may be your only option.

How are people going to find out about our digital ministry? No matter the type of application and features that you select, your potential audience must be able to find them! As you think through the goals of the ministry, one important point to consider is the method by which you expect people to find out about what you are doing. If you are hoping to expand your ministry and get in touch with new people, then you will need to consider how the technology you choose can be optimized for a higher ranking in search results. On the other hand, if your site is simply for those who already know you, then this may not be as important: you can always tell them about your site via an email or some other existing communication channel.

In the world of websites, optimizing your site so that people can find you is called *search engine optimization*, or SEO. There are many ways to improve your site's search ranking; some of these are free and simple, and others will require some real technical work. According to my best-practices research, 51 percent of ministries that took the time to do some SEO were successful, as compared to 25 percent success for those that did not.

If you are creating new streams using social media, the key to being found is remembering that it is all about relationships. Just as a friend's recommendation on what new restaurant to try is more valuable than any advertising, so is a social media mention for your ministry. Use digital technologies to tell a compelling story, and people will come to you.

How will we know if it is working? Another question to ask about technology is how you measure success. For each digital technology you utilize, you will want to set goals for how it is used, which implies that the tool must have a method for measuring its use! My research showed that this particular practice made a significant impact: 51 percent of ministries that collected data on their online efforts reported success, compared to only 16 percent for those that did not! *This is the single largest impact shown by the research.*

When deciding on which application you want to use for your ministry, you will want to understand how they track usage and if they can track the specific type of usage you have determined is important. For a website, this may simply be the number of *hits*, which represent how many people have looked at a page; for an app, it may be the number of downloads. But you may also want to know how long people have stayed on the page or which buttons on the app they have pressed. When selecting a technology, be sure that it is capable of keeping track of your goals.

GOOGLE ANALYTICS

One simple way to begin collecting statistics on your website is to install Google Analytics. Google Analytics is a free service offered by Google that will let you track just about anything imaginable about how your website is being used. Statistics tracked include: number of hits, search terms used to find your site, originating location of users on your site, average time on your site, the type of device used to access your site, most popular links on your site and what site referred them to you. Installing Google Analytics is relatively simple, although you will need someone with full access to your website code to do it.

One question people often ask when I recommend Google Analytics is whether your website will be sharing data with Google. All data shared with Google are shared anonymously; but if this concerns you, you can opt out. By choosing to opt out, you will not be participating in Google's benchmarking activities and will not be able to participate in some of the advanced advertising features. If you choose to install Google Analytics, you will have to make the right decision for your ministry on whether to share data with Google.

As I stated earlier: technology is not the hard part. I do understand that, for many, understanding technology does not come easily, and I sympathize. I believe, however, that technology decisions are not nearly as important as most ministries think. In many cases, which technology solutions you go with matter much, much less than how you resolve the issues surrounding the other two components of the digital ministry framework: *people* and *process*.

People

The people component of the framework incorporates all the individuals who are a part of your digital ministry and how they are going to be used as part of the digital presence you are developing. Unlike computers, people are not always predictable. (Okay, sometimes computers are not either!) It is very important to consider the impact that the digital ministry you are planning is going to have on those who are putting it into place. Here are some of the issues to consider.

Who is responsible for the digital ministry? One of the first questions you should ask about your digital ministry is, "Whose job is it?" Since you're the one reading this book, the answer very likely will be that it is you! Many times a digital ministry is added as something extra or new to a ministry, and it is not in anyone's job description to support or manage it. This is dangerous! It is crucial that a ministry designate one individual, preferably someone on staff, to be the responsible party for the digital ministry. This person does not have to know how to resolve all technical issues, but she or he can be the central point of contact for any problems with the ministry. This person should also be the one to ensure that the site is staying updated and on mission on a day-to-day basis.

According to my best-practices research, having one specific person responsible had a big impact on a digital ministry's success. Forty-nine percent of ministries that designated one person to be responsible for the digital aspects of their organization reported success, while only 22 percent of those who did not reported success.

Is there a team for planning and direction? While it is essential that one person be responsible for the online ministry, it is also important that there be a team of people who meet regularly and who set the direction for the digital ministry. A team of three to seven people, including the person with overall responsibility for the project, should be on this team. The team should also include at least one person from the ministry with decision-making authority. Do not make this an all-volunteer team! This team should not only help set direction but also should review the progress of the digital ministry in comparison to its goals. Again, the best-practices report supports this: 52 percent of ministries that had a team responsible for planning were successful, as compared to 31 percent success for those that did not.

Who will design and implement it? If you decide to create a new system, the next question becomes: who builds it? Should someone on staff build it? Should you hire out? How about a volunteer? Even when the system is purchased or built by an outside entity, someone inside the ministry will need to play a role in managing its implementation.

The first step to making this determination is to inventory the skill sets you have available on staff. If there is someone on staff who can build the system (and can spare their time to do it), then this may be a good option. If a staff member is unable to do so (or if you do not want their time spent on it), then it would make sense to see if you can bring in an outside consultant to do the work. Of course, for many ministries, this may present a problem due to budget constraints. In my opinion, however, this would be money well spent.

And what about using volunteers to build the site? My research shows that using volunteers is not a wise choice when it comes to building or implementing a system. The use of volunteers lowered reported success by 16 percent, while the use of internal staff raised success by 9 percent. In some cases, of course, using volunteers may be a ministry's only choice.

What is the role of volunteers? If, in general, a volunteer should not be used to build the system, what is the role of volunteers? My research shows that volunteers are best utilized with noncritical parts of the ministry. In other words, do not use volunteers for high-priority or time-sensitive parts of the project, such as building an application or being the primary support. Instead, use volunteers for parts of the project that are smaller and can be easily postponed or changed. For example, a volunteer could write noncritical content for the site or promote the site.

I realize that, for many ministries, the use of volunteers is critical to success. In fact, your ministry may be made up of 100 percent volunteers! To those for whom using volunteers is the only real choice: if you can identify highly reliable, skilled volunteers who are fully committed to your ministry, you should feel confident utilizing them. You should also be sure you have a structured process in place to manage these volunteers.

Who are the users? Perhaps the most important parts of the *people* component are those who will be the users of what you are creating. In order to build a relationship with someone, you have to know who they are. Have you taken some time to identify your target audience? This may be more difficult than you think. For example, if you are a church, will the users be existing members of the church or those in the community who are potential new congregants? For ministries: will the users be donors, clients or your volunteers? The simple (and lazy) answer would be "all of them." But this will lead to a fractured strategy. Identifying a primary user group and planning your strategy around that group is important. We will look at this more in the next chapter, so that is all I will say for now.

The third and final component of the digital ministry framework is *process*. Probably the most overlooked and least understood of the three components, process plays a critical role in the success of digital ministry.

Process

A process is a series of steps that must be completed in order to achieve a goal. An example of a process is how a church accepts new members or how an employee is hired. You have many processes in your ministry already, but are they documented and well understood? In order to have a successful digital ministry, you must get serious about processes. In fact, according to my best-practices research, *managing your processes well is the most important of the three components of the digital ministry framework.*

What kinds of processes are required for a digital ministry? From my research, I found that the most important processes are those surrounding the *planning* of the digital ministry. Processes involving the implementation and day-to-day use of the digital ministry are important, but they have a lower impact on success. Here are some of the questions to ask about processes.

Are there written, measurable goals and a mission statement? As you read in chapter 3, where we discussed how ministries can change, it is critical for your ministry to have a clear mission and goals. The digital component of your ministry should also have its own mission and goals. These goals should align with the overall ministry goals and should be clear enough to help the steering committee make decisions. Those ministries in my study that had a mission statement and/ or well-defined goals for their digital ministry were successful 45 percent of the time, as opposed to those ministries who did not have these goals in place, which had success 30 percent of the time.

What do I mean by *goals*? These goals should be explicit enough so that those guiding your ministry can determine whether the goal is being met. For example, a goal of a digital ministry could be: "to deepen the faith of anyone who visits our ministry website." This is a wonderful goal, but how can it be measured? Instead, the goal could read: "to move ten people a month from step one through step five of our spiritual maturity matrix." You could then track the usage of your website in such a way that you will know how people move through your process, and you could determine easily whether or not you are meeting your goal.

What do we know about our target audience? As part of your mission or goals, your digital ministry will have identified a group of people to be your users. Once you have identified these people, you need to know how to reach them. Many ministries simply stop here, thinking that they already know how to reach their target audience. This is not a good approach! It is imperative that you do some real research to understand their Internet habits and the feelings they have toward different approaches you might take. You can do this through a survey, focus groups or even third-party research such as the Pew Internet & American Life Project.

The research supports this: those ministries that did research on their users were identified as successful 52 percent of the time. Those that did not do this research succeeded only 26 percent of the time. With the exception of collecting data on the usage of the digital ministry (see the technology section of this chapter), this was the largest impact found by the research.

What is the process for making changes to the digital ministry? Once your digital ministry is in place, it is critical that you have a process for making changes to it. Who is allowed to do this, and how is it done? Is there centralized control, or will you allow anyone to update? Do you require an approval process before updating? Depending upon the goals for your ministry, you will want to strike a balance between strict centralized control (one person approves and updates everything) and a free-for-all (anyone can update anything). Generally, the more dynamic and changing the content, the more successful your digital ministry will be, but that could come at a price.

In my best-practices research on this topic, I found an apparent paradox. It turned out that *both* having a centralized approval process and allowing for distributed updates had positive effects on success! So what is the takeaway? Ministries will have to find a balance between maintaining quality through an approval process while also keeping their ministry dynamic by allowing selected members of their ministry to make changes.

An example of this would be a church website. Let's say that a congregation wants to maintain a high-quality website that meets very high standards, so they implement a strict update approval process. But the youth pastor wants to make updates several times a week to the high school youth group page and does not want to have to have someone approve every change. One way to resolve this conflict is to give the youth pastor his or her own blog page and/or a Facebook page that the youth pastor can update directly without approval. This could leave updates on the "official" church website under the centralized approval process.

Do we provide training? Another process to think about is training. Once you have your digital ministry in place, will those who use it need to be trained? Many times, this is left out of the planning, but it could be crucial to success. And training is not just teaching someone how to use a technology; it is also teaching someone what the correct processes are for making changes to the site or posting content. Again, the research supports this: ministries that provided training on the use of their digital ministry reported success 42 percent of the time, compared to 32 percent of the time for ministries that did not.

Managing your digital ministry processes will have the biggest impact on the success of your digital ministry. It is also the component of the digital ministry framework that will take the most effort and organizational support.

Putting It All Together

So how can you apply this digital ministry framework to your own ministry? What if you already have a digital ministry going and realize now that you have not paid attention to one of the three components? What is your next step?

The next two chapters will walk you through the steps of developing and implementing a digital ministry strategy. Whether you are just starting out or you have had a ministry in place for a while, this strategy road map will help you develop a comprehensive, written strategy that you can use to create or improve your digital ministry.

5

Planning Your Digital Strategy

Strategy forces us to seek the mind and will of God.
Strategy is an attempt to anticipate the future God wants
to bring about. It is a statement of faith as to what we believe that
future to be and how we can go about bringing it into existence.

Edward R. Dayton and David Allen Fraser,
Planning Strategies for World Evangelization[1]

While the majority of ministries now use the Internet and other digital technologies in some form, most have never bothered to develop a strategy to do so. In previous chapters, we have reviewed some of the foundational principles behind the development of a digital strategy. In this chapter we will begin looking at the steps your ministry can take to develop a digital strategy. This strategy approach is based on the digital ministry framework and incorporates many of the ideas that have been covered in the past few chapters.

What Is a Strategy?

The first step to developing a strategy is to be sure that you understand what it means to have a strategy. Many people within organizations think they have a strategy when, in fact, they have simply decided that they are going to use Facebook and start a blog. This is not a strategy.

So then what is strategy? In his book, *Media in Church and Mission,* Viggo Søgaard writes,

> Strategy is a way to reach an objective, a kind of map of the territory to be covered in order to 'reach from here to there.' Strategy is a conceptual way of anticipating the future, guiding us in major decisions concerning alternative approaches and decisive action. In this way strategy helps us by providing a sense of direction and cohesiveness, focusing on the central issues of our task and philosophy of ministry. . . . We could also say that Christian communication strategy is the process of planning with an aim to align our plans with God's plans, seeking his will for us and our ministry.[2]

Using this definition as a starting point, this chapter will help you begin developing a digital ministry strategy for your own organization.

Is Strategy Biblical?

Churches and ministries have sometimes shied away from the need for strategy. I have found that most ministries want to skip the planning process altogether and get straight to the implementation. "Can't we let God just lead us?" is the refrain I often hear. Yet this is shortsighted. In my opinion, this is simply the response of someone afraid to move outside their comfort zone. The Lord expects us to use the resources given us wisely, which requires us to do effective planning.

In his book, Søgaard points out several biblical examples of strategy. First, he notes that God seems to be following a strategic method in dealing with humanity. God called Abraham, a specific person, so that he might bless all nations through him (Genesis 12:3, Galatians 3:8). Then he called a specific nation, Israel, at specific times for specific purposes. He sent his Son at a specific time in history for a specific purpose (Ephesians 1:9-10). When Christ was on this earth, Jesus used a similar strategy, selecting a small and specific group of people (Mark 3:13-19), training them and sending them out with a specific commission (Matthew 28:18-20). Finally, the Holy Spirit selected certain people at specific times for specific goals, like Paul to go to the Gentiles (Acts 9:15).

Another example given by Søgaard is from 1 Chronicles. When King David was planning to go to war, he brought in strategists from Issachar, men who "understood the times and knew what Israel should do" (1 Chronicles 12:32). The same should be said for our ministries. We need to be aware of the current trends and issues in our culture so we can know how to develop a strategy!

Strategy Gives Us Confidence

We are in a time of unprecedented change. Those in ministry who are trying to use the Internet can see their well-laid plans become outdated before they even get started. How can we be confident that the plans we make for a digital ministry will be successful? Sometimes it seems as if we are trying to hit a moving target. If your ministry has a well-thought-out digital strategy, however, you need not be afraid of changing technologies, because you will have a process in place to deal with changes in technology.

Another way strategy can bring you confidence is by giving you a method for dealing with the myriad of technologies available to your ministry. We can get paralyzed by the sheer number of choices. Should we create a blog? What about a mobile app? Should we do video? How about social network integration? Can we somehow use Twitter? And what about letting people "check in" when they come to our church?

No ministry should expect to do everything. Again, having a solid strategy in place will give you a method to determine which tools are the right ones to use and will give you confidence in how you are using them. Maybe more importantly, a strategy will also help you determine what you should *not* do. In this and the following chapter, you will learn how to develop a strategy that will give you a solid, well-thought-out approach to using digital tools for your ministry.

Who and How?

Before you get started on strategy development for your digital ministry, you should first identify a team of committed individuals to help develop it. My suggestion is that the team should stay small—around three to five individuals—with no more than one or two people who are not on the paid staff of the ministry. All of the individuals on the team should be completely committed to the mission of the ministry and the idea of digital ministry.

To answer the question "How long will this take?" I usually answer, "It depends." Since that is not a satisfactory answer for most people, let's delve a little deeper. Putting together a strategy for a digital ministry and getting it up and running can take anywhere from a month to a year, depending upon a variety of factors: how often your team can meet, the goals you have for your digital ministry and the availability of resources, among other issues. Many ministry leaders want to rush through the strategy development process or skip it altogether, but this has the potential to lead to a digital ministry implementation that is shortsighted or ill-formed.

A Strategic Model for Digital Ministry

In his book *Media in Church and Mission,* Viggo Søgaard presents a strategy model adapted from *Planning Strategies for World Evangelization* by Edward R. Dayton and David Allen Fraser. This model was originally developed in 1980 and later revised in 1993. I have taken this model and further modified it for use in the development of a strategy for digital ministry. It is a circular model containing thirteen steps, with the thirteenth step being to start over and do it again.

Using this model as a starting point and integrating the digital ministry framework and the results of my best-practices research, I have developed the following set of steps that can be used to develop a digital ministry strategy.

1. Define the purpose and objectives for the use of the digital tools by your ministry.

2. Describe the target group(s) for your digital ministry.

3. Research your target group(s)' use of digital technologies.

4. Determine the resources available.

5. Create a list of possible solutions.

6. Select the tools you will use.

7. Plan for the implementation and operation of your digital ministry.

8. Forecast results.

9. Assign roles and responsibilities.

10. Write it up!

11. Carry out the plan.

12. Evaluate results.

13. Do it again!

A Strategic Model: Steps One Through Six

Let's look at each of these steps in a little detail. We'll look at the first six steps in this chapter, and then at the last seven steps in the next chapter.

Step 1: Define the purpose and objectives for the use of the digital tools by your ministry. The first step toward developing a strategy for digital ministry is to develop a mission statement for your use of digital technologies. *This mission statement should be fully aligned with your own organization's mission statement but should be specific to the use of the digital tools.*

In order to create a successful digital ministry, you must first know who you are! You must understand what your organization is about; from there, you can determine how you will leverage digital technologies. Remember, *just using digital tools is not a strategy in itself.* Some pointers about developing a mission statement follow.

- It should be relatively short (one to two sentences) and memorable.

- It should be able to provide direction for decision making about the project.

- It should be specific enough to limit your use of digital technologies, allowing you to focus on your overall ministry goals.

- It should not contain the specifics on which technologies you will use.

- It should be in complete alignment with the mission of your organization. (If you don't have a mission for your ministry, then stop here and develop that before going on.)

An example of a poor digital ministry mission statement would be: "We will use YouTube to carry out the mission of our ministry more effectively." This statement does not really say anything except that you will use YouTube. How did you decide that YouTube was the right solution? Your mission statement should not specify a technology!

An example of a good mission statement is: "Our ministry will use digital technologies to strengthen the faith of youth in the Los Angeles area through the development of culturally relevant online materials. Further, we hope to use these tools to build and strengthen relationships between those youth and our partner churches." This statement is both informative and limiting. It also focuses on a key point made earlier in this book: *using digital tools should be about building relationships.*

If you have two or three separate purposes for your use of digital technologies (such as a church reaching *in* to its own members and also reaching *out* to its community), it may be wise to develop two or more separate projects with two separate mission statements and then prioritize which project should be done first. While both may be admirable, it will lead to conflicts down the line if you are trying to accomplish projects with separate and distinct missions.

Once you have developed a good mission statement for the project, you are ready to move on to the next step, which is identifying your target users.

Step 2: Describe the target group(s) for your digital ministry. For this step, you should define as specifically as possible the group of people to whom your digital ministry will be directed. These are your "target users." The more specific you can be, the better you can tailor your online ministry to reach this group. If your mission leads you to target more than one group of people, then you will want to make that clear. If the groups are quite distinct from each other, then (as with the mission statement) it may be best to create more than one project and tackle them in a prioritized order. Some questions to ask about your target user include the following.

- What age or age range are they?
- What stage of life are they in?
- What gender are they?
- Where are they located physically?
- What faith group are they from?
- How mature is their faith?
- Do they have any characteristics in common?

Note that you do not need to specify all of the above characteristics, but if you leave too many of them blank, you are probably targeting too large an audience. The more you focus on a particular group, the better you can plan your digital ministry.

Step 3: Research your target group(s)' use of digital technologies. Once you have identified your potential audience, it is essential that you fully understand their digital habits. This is where so many go wrong: they assume that they already understand their audience and can skip this step. *Simply using intuition or a "gut feeling" about it is not acceptable; you must include solid research on your target audience as part of your strategic planning.*

Research is important for two reasons. First, it will help you understand the best way to reach your target audience. If you design your research well, you will come up with new insights about your target users that will surprise you. For example, when I worked with a church on a website project a couple of years ago, we first did a survey of the congregation to understand their usage and attitudes toward the Internet. Going in, we had an assumption that our congregants over sixty would want very little to do with the Internet, and we were already planning on how to handle that. But were we ever wrong! The usage of the Internet and email were just as high by people in their sixties as they were by people in their twenties. Knowing this allowed us to include more things online and to feel confident that we could reach the majority of the church.

The second reason research is important is simple: funding. If your ministry is applying for a grant or needs approval for funding from a board or oversight committee, you stand a much better chance of gaining approval if you can show solid research that supports your decisions. Good research will give you the ability to defend your strategy in front of those from whom you will be asking for resources.

You can go about research several different ways. Let me suggest three: surveys, focus groups and third-party data. If possible, directly surveying your target group is probably the best way to understand them. Creating a well-thought-out survey is not simple; I would suggest that, if possible, you find a survey used by a reputable research organization and modify it, as opposed to creating one yourself. I have included a copy of a survey that I used when doing research at my own church a few years ago, available as appendix C.

Another research method is focus groups. If you can get a group of individuals from your target group together to discuss how they use digital tools, you will learn quite a bit about how to reach them. A focus group is more than simply having coffee with people; for a focus group, you need to have specific goals in mind before beginning.

Finally, using third-party data, such as that from the Pew Internet & American Life Project or the U.S. Census, will also give you some ideas of how to reach your group. If possible, combine two or three of these methods to help you fully understand your target group.

THE PEW INTERNET & AMERICAN LIFE PROJECT

One extremely valuable resource for doing research on the digital habits of your target group is the Pew Internet & American Life Project. Founded in late 1999, the project aims to document the use of the Internet by Americans and to study how that use affects our daily lives. With hundreds of studies and articles now available, this resource can be an important component for your research. All reports and data collected on the site are free. You may even download the original surveys used and do your own analysis on all of the data. You can access the project at pewinternet.org.

CASE STUDY:
FIRST CHURCH'S HIGH SCHOOL MINISTRY

Allen Kim is the youth pastor at First Church. He is excited to use Facebook and Twitter as a way to connect with the members of his youth group. Following the digital ministry framework, he knows that he needs to understand his goals for the use of digital technologies before jumping in and using them for ministry purposes. In a meeting with the pastor and a church elder, he was able to develop a mission statement for the church high school youth group's use of digital technologies: "The First Church Youth Ministry will use digital technologies to connect with local high school students through the devices they use on a daily basis. We endeavor to disciple these students on a daily basis as they seek to deepen their faith."

Using this mission statement as a starting point, Allen then worked to identify the demographics of the target user as follows.

- They are students at one of the two high schools in the same city as the church.
- They are in ninth through twelfth grade, with a focus on ninth and tenth grade.
- They currently attend a youth group event at least once a month.
- They have generally come to faith through their parents or First Church but have not devoted much time to deepening their faith.

Using this demographic information, Allen then does research. He starts by accessing the U.S. Census data about the demographics of the city in which the church is located. He confirms his beliefs that the residents of the city are primarily middle- to upper-class and that it has a high percentage of households with children. He is surprised to find that the city is 34 percent Hispanic; his youth group has only one or two Hispanic students and is primarily white and Asian.

After reviewing census data, he turns his attention to the Pew Internet & American Life Project. Here, he finds research indicating that 75 percent of teens have mobile phones, and that those numbers get higher as they get older. He also finds that while 80 percent of teens are on Facebook, only 16 percent use Twitter, with both numbers continuing to trend higher. This leads him to reconsider his idea to use Twitter.

Armed with this initial research, Allen will now develop an online survey and ask all of his youth group members to take it. He will then use those results to shape his strategy and select the appropriate tools and policies in the upcoming steps.

Step 4: Determine the resources available. At this point, you have determined the mission and goals for your online strategy, and you have identified and developed a good understanding of the people for whom you are developing it. But before you can start selecting specific technologies, you have one more step to complete: determining your available resources. In order to create an effective online ministry, you must understand your own capacity to implement and maintain it. The resources you have will determine that.

What do I mean by resources? There are three primary categories of resources: skills, available time and money.

1. *Skills*. The first thing to do is to inventory the skills available to your organization. These can be both technical and nontechnical skills, and your need for these skills will vary depending upon your project's goals. Some technical skills to consider include:

- programming
- website development skills
- technical knowledge of specific software programs
- graphic design

  Some nontechnical skills to consider include:

- writing ability
- editing expertise
- general business understanding
- research skills
- project management
- marketing ability

Identifying who has a detailed understanding of the ministry is also important. Perhaps the most important but often overlooked nontechnical skill is the ability to work effectively with people. Understanding how to communicate, read between the lines, resolve conflicts and influence behavior are crucial skills that every digital ministry will need to have represented. At this point, you are not assigning people to the project as much as identifying the full range of skills that your ministry has available.

As discussed in the previous chapter, it will be critical to differentiate the skills you have available from staff members of the organization and the skills available from volunteers. Again, a ministry should be wary of using volunteers for mission-critical parts of the project, such as the development of a website.

2. *Available time*. The next resource category to consider is available time. Even if you identified some great skills in the previous category, your ability to utilize them may be hampered by the fact that the person with the skill just cannot commit the time or the fact that the ministry can't give them up for this project. If you have identified one or more people to devote to this project, are you willing to have them take time from their normal duties to work on it?

3. *Money*. When undertaking a project such as this, most ministries already have a firm grasp of the amount of funding available. Obviously, knowing this will be an important factor in making an informed choice for software or tools you will use for the ministry.

Financial resources can be used to purchase software or pay for a consultant to build software or assist with the overall project. A full discussion of how to best manage a consultant goes beyond the scope of this book, but there are some things to consider. First of all, be sure that all expectations are fully documented in a written agreement before the consulting work begins. This will eliminate frustration and disagreements down the line. If possible, have someone who has previously worked with a technology consultant review the contract to be sure that all aspects are covered. Second, be sure that the consultant can educate you so that you are not forced to continue to call him or her over and over again after the work is completed.

If a consultant cannot be found—or, more likely, if you do not have the money available to hire one—then you may need to consider a volunteer for this role. It is critical that the volunteer be someone you can rely on and who fully understands the mission of the organization and the project.

Step 5: Create a list of possible solutions. If your ministry is like most, you will be anxious to begin selecting the digital technologies you will use before you have done any of the preceding steps. Until you have developed the project's mission, understood your target users and made an inventory of your available resources, however, you won't be able to make an informed choice about the tools you will be using.

So how do you go about selecting technology? I would suggest that you start by going back to your mission statement and goals to determine the functions that it should have. Combine these requirements with the results of your research on your target user to come up with a list of the essential functions. Your mission statement and goals should also help you limit the functions you need. Your list of essential functions should be somewhat brief, with only five to ten functions listed.

Once you have created this list, you can start to compare different digital tools against this list. Now, let me state that it is nearly impossible to determine what *all* of the possible tools are. Instead, you want to be sure you have thought through the different *categories* of tools that you could use.

What do I mean by a tool category? There are dozens of different categories of digital tools, each with different functions. By using categories instead of brand names, you are working to keep your personal biases at arm's length. Examples of tool categories include blogs, podcasts, websites, social networks and photo sharing. Because technology changes constantly, it is impossible to know all of the tool categories, let alone all the possible tools. Keeping abreast of the latest technologies is so important; it takes work to keep up. To aid you in getting started in this process, you will find a list of some of the more popular digital tool categories in appendix A.

Try to identify as many different categories of tools as possible that meet one or more of the functions you will require. Get input from many different sources, and see if you can think outside the box. Once you have developed this list of possible solutions, you can then move on to the step of selecting the best digital technologies for your ministry.

Step 6: Select the tools you will use. We are now at the point at which you can begin the final selection process of your technologies. You will start by comparing the different categories of technologies you identified and determining which one(s) best meet your needs. For each category of technology, you will want to identify which of your required functions it meets, along with your ability to implement it based upon your available resources. This can be quite a difficult process.

One method that I would highly recommend is using an evaluation matrix. You can set up this matrix to compare the requirements for the tools with the categories of digital technologies you have come up with. This matrix should list the technologies along the side and the required features across the top. Table 5.1 is an example of how this matrix might look.

Table 5.1. Digital Tool Evaluation Matrix

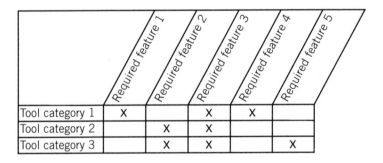

	Required feature 1	Required feature 2	Required feature 3	Required feature 4	Required feature 5
Tool category 1	X		X	X	
Tool category 2		X	X		
Tool category 3		X	X		X

After you have made a decision about the category of tool you will use, then you can look at different tools within that category and choose the one that meets your criteria the best. In some cases, there will be one tool in a category that is obvious; in other cases, you may have to review several tools before making a decision. To see how this all plays out, take a look at the case of the fictitious Christian Growth Ministries.

CASE STUDY:
CHRISTIAN GROWTH MINISTRIES (CGM)

CGM is a grassroots missions organization that wants to help young people become more rooted in their faith. They have already completed the first five steps of the digital strategy framework and have come up with the following.

- *Project mission:* "to educate new Christians on the core beliefs of the faith through the use of the Nicene Creed."
- *Target audience:* new Christians on college campuses within the United States.
- *Research:* 98 percent of their target audience use Facebook, 99 percent use email and 33 percent have smartphones.
- *Resources:* no money (all part-time volunteers), no one with web development skills and several people with three to five hours a week to commit to the project.

After reviewing their situation, CGM has decided that their online ministry will need: the ability to clearly communicate the Nicene Creed in multiple formats (text, audio, video); the ability to build relationships by identifying the people they are working with; the ability to integrate email and/or Facebook easily; and to be easy enough to use that no training is required. Of course, since they have no money, it must be free as well. And since they do not have access to technical resources, it must be something that their existing team can manage to use.

In reviewing what other ministries have done, several categories of solutions come to mind: using a social network, creating a blog, building a website, creating a podcast, creating online videos, or even just an email campaign. Taking these categories of solutions and running them against their required functions, they developed an evaluation matrix as shown here:

Required Function

Tool Category	Ability to communicate in multiple formats	Clearly identify users	Integrate with email	Integrate with Facebook	No training required	Free	Can be supported by existing staff
Social Network	X	X		X	X	X	X
Blog	X		X	X	X	X	X
Website	X		X	X			
Podcast							
Online Video			X				
Mobile App	X	X					

Figure 5.2. Digital Tool Evaluation Matrix for CGM

After reviewing their analysis, the choice becomes pretty clear: social networking software and blogging both meet almost all of the criteria, followed by a website. Based on their research, their target users were big users on social networks, specifically Facebook. Due to limited resources, the team decided to wait on implementing a blog or a website until after the Facebook ministry was implemented.

Technology Is Not the Hard Part

These first steps have focused primarily on the technology component of the digital ministry framework. In many ways, these are the easiest parts of putting together a digital ministry: identifying your needs and selecting technology. The harder parts are yet to come: implementing the technology and putting the appropriate people and processes in place. We will cover those steps in the next chapter.

6

Implementing and Running Your Digital Ministry

All hard work brings a profit, but mere talk leads only to poverty.

Proverbs 14:23

In the previous chapter, we looked at exactly what it means to have a strategy for your digital ministry and how to develop a method for selecting the proper technology tools. Using a strategy model that incorporated the digital ministry framework, we went through the first six steps of the process, which took us from the development of a mission statement for the digital ministry up to the point of selecting the software tools.

I stated at the end of that chapter that, in many ways, everything up to that point was easy compared to what was to come. Many ministries, having gotten to the point of selecting their digital tools, are then completely ineffective with the implementation and operation of those tools. In this chapter, we go through the completion of the strategy, which focuses on how to implement and maintain your digital ministry.

A Strategic Model: Steps Seven Through Thirteen

Before we begin reviewing these steps, let me point out that, while the steps in the previous chapter should be completed in order, *some of the steps discussed in this chapter can be completed in any order or even at the same time.* Specifically, the first three steps in this chapter (steps seven, eight and nine) can be done in any order. Many times, while doing one of these three steps, you will find that working on the other steps will feel quite natural. Feel free to do so—as long as you complete all three steps before moving on to step ten.

Step 7: Plan for the implementation and operation of your digital ministry. Once you have determined which technologies you will be using, you must develop the policies and procedures you need to get your digital ministry up and running. There is no quick fix or cookie-cutter solution here. *This step takes time and will most likely require several iterations before you have a complete document.*

While the exact processes each ministry uses are not the same, the categories of processes are similar. These processes can be categorized by the stage at which they take place. Processes that occur as part of the implementation of the digital ministry generally will only happen once, for a set period of time. This includes things like coming up with the design and layout of any pages or screens and the actual creation of any websites or content. Processes that are part of the support and ongoing operations of the digital ministry will occur on a regular basis for as long as the ministry continues. This difference is important. Activities that occur only once can be planned to occur at a particular time, and resources can be allocated on a one-time basis. Many times, it makes sense to pay for one-time activities instead of interrupting the flow of work in your organization. For activities related to the day-to-day support and operation of the digital ministry, you will need to allocate resources on an ongoing basis. Let's take a look at some of the activities for which you will need to plan.

Implementation (One-Time Activities)

- *Digital ministry design.* How will your digital ministry work, and what will it look like? If you are using a ministry "brand" or logo, who needs to approve its use? Does the digital tool you selected allow you to customize the way it works or looks? Are there any privacy or security issues you should consider as you design how it will work? It is important to consider these questions and develop a procedure for how they will be addressed before you begin development with the tools themselves.

- *Digital ministry development.* Will your staff develop this? A consultant? If software development is required, who will manage it? Even if you chose to go with a solution that does not require you to build anything new, some customization may be required. How will you decide when it is completed? Have you written a full description of what you want it to do? How will you know when you are ready to launch?

- *Digital ministry launch.* How will you launch your ministry? Will you do any marketing? Is any training needed? Does everyone have what they need to get started? Does everyone understand their roles? Have you done some real testing on the site? It is in this stage that you figure out how to get your new digital ministry into your target users' "stream" (see chapter 2).

Operations (Day-to-Day)

- *Digital ministry support.* Who is the one point of contact at your ministry for your online presence? Who will that person contact if something goes wrong? Can they fix it themselves? Who has the authority to take the site down or disable it if necessary? If you are working with a vendor or consultant on this, do you understand their support policies? Is it clear to the users how to contact you if something is not working? A broken website or app is one that users will abandon quickly.

- *Privacy and security policies.* As part of the planning process, ensure that you protect the privacy of those using your digital ministry and that you secure your ministry's digital resources. This is such an important topic that an entire chapter (chapter 7) discusses the possible issues surrounding these topics.

- *Digital ministry maintenance.* Once your digital ministry is up and running, what needs to be done to keep it going? Who will update the website? How often should updates be done? Who will monitor comments or posts? How many hours a week should be devoted to the digital ministry? This is an extremely important category of processes to develop; many ministries lose focus at this point because it is "done."

- *Oversight.* A final category to consider is oversight. Who will review the online ministry to determine if it is actually meeting its goals and fulfilling its mission? How often should this group meet? What statistics should be collected, and how will that be accomplished? What criteria will you use to determine success? And what will cause you to reconsider what you are doing?

Let me make a point here about keeping content updated. Nothing derails a digital ministry more than irrelevant or low-quality content. If you are going to have a Facebook page, blog or some other sort of digital presence, you must keep your content updated, accurate and interesting. The best way to do this is to empower those closest to the ministry to do the updating. For example: if you have a Facebook page for your church's women's ministry, then someone in the leadership of the women's ministry should do the updating. This person has the most relevant content and the most incentive to keep the page updated.

At the same time, however, you need to maintain quality. If the person who is the obvious choice for updating will not be able to do it or will not be able to produce quality content, then another solution must be found. Many organizations will hire someone part-time or full-time to maintain and/or edit content.

These processes are extremely important to the success of your online ministry. You should not rush through this seventh step but should give it *at least* as much consideration as the selection of the tool!

Once you have developed these processes, be sure you have them documented somewhere (see step ten). Make them available to everyone who needs them. Ideally, these processes will be written into the job descriptions of those who perform them to make it absolutely clear that these tasks are now part of their jobs. During performance reviews or annual evaluations, the support for the online ministry should play a prominent role.

Before we move to the next step, you should stop and ask this question: are we still confident in the choices we have made to this point? Has the creation of the processes we need to get the ministry up and running made us reconsider if we will be able to commit to this? Are we trying to do too much? If you think so, it may be a good time to review the choices to this point and see where you can scale back. Maybe your original goals were too lofty.

CASE STUDY:
SECOND CHURCH WOMEN'S MINISTRY

In my best-practices research, I found that allowing the people closest to a webpage's content to also be responsible for updating it works best. I call this distributed updating. It is the opposite of the centralized updating model, in which one person makes all the updates to the webpage.

Consider the fictitious example of Second Church of

Anytown, USA. Second Church is relatively small except for its women's ministries program. Over one hundred women come from all over the community every week to attend events sponsored by this ministry. For this church, the women's ministry is a great outreach opportunity.

The leaders of the women's ministry decided that they needed to get their ministry into the digital age. After working through the strategic planning process outlined here, they decided to start a ministry blog. The digital ministry team for this project has set a goal of posting one inspirational message per day to the blog, along with any news or updates about events for the ministry. This blog also will update a Facebook page that they have created, so that between the blog and the Facebook page, they should be able to reach almost all the women in the ministry and (hopefully) continue to grow.

But now the question: who keeps the blog updated? When the digital ministry team discusses it, they come up with three candidates.

- The leader of the women's ministry. This person is a full-time church staff member but is reluctant to commit her time to making these updates.
- A member of the women's ministry who is a volunteer leader. This person has some web experience and has been coming to the events for a couple of years. She is the one who started the Facebook page.
- The church secretary. This person currently updates the church website once a week but does not attend the women's ministry programs.

Who would you choose?

Ideally, the leader of women's ministries would do it or would delegate it to one of her staff. Having a volunteer do it is risky, but this person could be given a trial run to see how it goes. If the volunteer does do it, the women's ministry leader should, as part of her job, monitor that it is getting done. Having the church secretary do it would probably work, but this person cannot be expected to write an inspirational message on a daily basis. If the goal of the daily message is removed, then having the church secretary update the blog with event information and news would probably make sense. Again, though, someone from the ministry would need to make sure it is getting done.

Let's say that the church chose to allow the volunteer to do it, with oversight from the women's ministry leader. They are still going to shoot for one inspirational post a day, along with announcements and events. They come up with the following policy for blog updating.

The blog will be updated by a designated volunteer on a daily basis. On a daily basis, this person will post a biblically based inspirational message. This message should appear no later than 3:00 p.m. each day, Monday through Friday, and should be at least one hundred words long. This person will also post announcements about ministry events and any news related to the ministry. The designated volunteer will meet once every two weeks with the women's ministry leader to review the postings and to come up with ideas for future postings. It will be the women's ministry leader's responsibility to ensure that the blog is getting updated.

Step 8: Forecast results. This step involves dreaming a little. You and your team should sit back and think how you would answer the question: if our digital ministry were fully successful, what would that look like? Using the digital tools you have chosen, the people involved and the processes you will put in place, what would be the best possible result? What would be acceptable? In order for your ministry to be considered a success, it should be fulfilling its mission. Therefore, these results, if reached, should show that your ministry has in fact met the goals you developed in step one.

Part of strategic planning is also accepting the cold, hard reality that you might fail. In order to understand if you are succeeding or failing, you must be able to measure your results and compare them to some success indicator. This means that you cannot choose your success criteria to be something such as "bringing people closer to Christ" or "increasing awareness of our ministry." While these are wonderful goals, they fail to include two key attributes of success indicators: they must be *measurable* and they must be *specific*.

A measurable result is one that can be determined by looking at statistics. It is likely that the digital tools you chose already have the ability to collect information: number of people who have visited the website, buttons that were clicked in the app, length of time that people used it, number of comments posted, etc. Your goals can also include the softer, not so easily measurable goals as described above, but you will really have no way to measure them.

Once you have identified your goals, you need to be sure that the digital tools you selected have a way to measure them. If not, you may need to include some sort of third-party statistics package, such as the free Google Analytics, as part of your software solution. If there is no real way to collect statistics about your digital ministry, then you may need to consider changing the software you have selected.

A specific result is one that puts hard numbers to the statistics you are measuring. This generally includes identifying a specific number within a designated period of time. For example, "Our website will receive fifty hits per day on average after six months," or "One thousand people will download our app in the first six months." The difficult part is in identifying exactly what these numerical goals should be. My suggestion is to look at some of the numbers that other ministries are seeing, if possible, and then determine where your ministry should fit in. You also may want to develop a range of values.

Once you have identified what success will look like for your digital ministry, take a moment to go back to your original goals and mission. Are they in line? Do you have at least one measurable result for each part of your mission? Are you being realistic about the goals you have set, and will it be possible to meet them?

MEASURABLE GOALS

Here are some examples of statistics that a ministry could measure to define a successful digital ministry.

Number of hits. This statistic is useful for determining how popular your ministry website is. If one of your goals is to increase awareness of your ministry, this one is a great choice.

Number of specific clicks. If you have a specific place on your ministry website to which you are trying to drive people (such as a link or button representing some sort of commitment), you can measure how many times viewers click on it.

Number of views. If your ministry is using an online video, then tracking how many times it is viewed all the way through is a great strategy for determining success.

Bounce rate. The "bounce rate" is the percentage of single-page visits to your website. Put another way, the bounce rate measures how many people come to your website and leave before doing anything. If your goal is for people to stay on your website and drill down into your content, then this is an important measure.

Most popular pages. This will let you know what website pages people are visiting the most and help you determine if a particular piece of content is being viewed.

Number of downloads. If you are creating a mobile app for your ministry, then you may want to set a goal for the number of downloads in a certain time period. This will also work if you are distributing something (such as a sermon series or video) that is being downloaded.

Search engine ranking. You can search for your website in the popular search engines and see where you rank. There are several things you can do to make a website show up higher in the search engine rankings.

Number of members. If your website or app allows people to create IDs (for example, for a discussion board or to access additional content), then you could track the number of people who do so.

Number of comments. If your website, video or blog allows for comments, then the number of comments you get can be measured. This is a good measure of how seriously people are taking your content and how interactive you are being.

Number/amount of donations. Keeping track of the number or amount of donations (or even the number of different people who donate) is definitely a way to measure how successful your online ministry is.

Step 9: Assign roles and responsibilities. As I stated at the beginning of this chapter, steps seven, eight and nine can be done in any order or even at the same time. It is here in step nine where you identify the specific people who will be working on your project. Most likely, you have already determined many of those who will be involved in the project, but this is the time to finalize it.

To do this, look over the processes you have developed and be sure you have people assigned to each process you have created. Who is involved in design? Who will be developing it? Who is involved in updating the site? Do they need to be trained? Again, the more of these people who are on staff with the ministry, the better.

Contact person. In addition to assigning people to the processes, you will also want to be sure you have identified the person who will be the point of contact for the digital ministry once it is up and running. This person does *not* have to be the person who will post content or actually fix problems when they occur. This is the person who has the authority to make decisions about the digital ministry and knows how to get in contact with the appropriate person when there are problems. This person should be on staff and have some authority to ensure that the site continues to function on a day-to-day basis.

Digital ministry oversight team. During this step you will finalize the team of people who are responsible for monitoring and reviewing the digital ministry's progress in the upcoming months. This team should consist of three to five people and should include the point person mentioned above, as well as at least one person from the ministry who is in senior leadership and has decision-making authority. This team should meet regularly, with meetings coming more often at first and then settling into an appropriate schedule. For example, the team could meet weekly during the implementation of the project and the first few weeks of operation and then move to a monthly meeting once things are running smoothly. It is likely, though not necessary, that some or all of the members of this team will have been on the team that developed the digital strategy.

The responsibilities of this team include providing oversight and guidance to the digital ministry. The team should also be responsible for

- reviewing the statistics being collected and comparing them to the goals of the ministry.

- making decisions, based on how the ministry is meeting its goals, regarding any changes that need to be made.

- scanning the environment to see if there are new technologies that should be considered for the ministry.

- reviewing any problems that the digital ministry is having.

- reviewing requested changes to the digital ministry and approving or denying them based upon the original mission and goals.

- determining when it is time to revise the mission of the digital ministry and make changes or, possibly, shut down the digital ministry.

Step 10: Write it up! After steps seven, eight and nine are completed, it is time to do the step that usually gets missed: putting the entire plan in writing. A written document detailing all the decisions you have made to this point will be useful for several reasons. First, it is a way of ensuring that everyone agrees on what has been decided upon to this point. This document can be sent out to all members of the team for review, ensuring that all members of the team have a complete understanding of the decisions made.

Having this document will also be useful as a way to bring people who join the project at a later date up to speed. It will also be the repository for all the written procedures that you developed in step seven; if someone is unsure of what the process is, they can refer to the document. This document will also make clear which people are responsible for the different processes.

Finally, this document can be used as a way to gain support from your board or constituents or anyone to whom you might be looking for funding. By fully documenting your strategy, you will be able to demonstrate that your online ministry is based on a well-thought-out, research-based strategy. This, in turn, may lead to more funding and better support for the project.

SAMPLE OUTLINE OF STRATEGY WRITEUP

Project Name:

Strategy Team:

Date:

1. Mission Statement
2. Target Audience
3. Tools Reviewed
4. Evaluation Criteria Used
5. Tools Selected
6. Roles and Responsibilities
7. Procedure Guide
   a. Design, development and implementation
   b. Day-to-day operations
   c. Oversight
8. Metrics

Step 11: Carry out the plan. At this point, you are ready to get started with your digital ministry. Most likely, you already have begun playing with the software and getting contracts in place. It is important that you do not skip any of the steps along the way, such as writing up processes, creating goals and researching users. Each of these steps plays a role in the long-term success of the project.

To kick off your digital ministry, I recommend that you identify two key players: a project champion and a project manager. Most likely, both of these individuals have already been a part of the project, but it will be important to identify both of these people.

A *project champion* is someone within the ministry who is part of leadership (ideally part of senior leadership) and is easily recognizable by the rest of the organization. This person should make clear her or his support for the project to the rest of the ministry. This will legitimize the project to everyone involved and give incentive to the team to prioritize the project.

The *project manager* is the person who oversees the day-to-day tasks necessary to implement the project. This person is responsible for keeping everyone on track, communicating progress to the rest of the team and ensuring that everyone has what they need to complete their tasks. This person will also keep the project schedule updated. It is not necessary that this be the same person identified in step nine as the person in charge of the digital ministry, although it could be.

I would suggest using some project management tools to keep track of the different facets of the project. Project communication could be managed through a project blog or webpage. Depending upon the complexity of the project, a more formal project management tool, such as Microsoft Project, may be needed.

As with any project, this project should have a start date and a planned end date. The project formally will end when the digital ministry is implemented and can be moved to day-to-day operations. The team should make clear what criteria will be used to determine that the project is completed.

Step 12: Evaluate results. Once your digital ministry is up and running, you will want to begin evaluating its effectiveness. Your oversight team should begin meeting on a regular basis; it is their responsibility to review the progress of the ministry in comparison to its goals.

The importance of this step should not be overlooked. It is this team's responsibility to make sure that the ministry stays on track. This team should review all of the data collected about the use of the digital ministry and compare those results to the goals set.

It is important to remember that your new digital ministry might not be successful—or at least not as successful as you were hoping. This oversight team will determine if the ministry should change or, even more importantly, if the digital ministry should not continue. Your ministry only has a limited amount of resources available, and you must determine if you are using them responsibly.

Step 13: Do it again! At some point in the life of your digital ministry, it will be time to reevaluate what you are doing and to determine what changes should be made. It may be six months, one year or three years after your initial implementation, but at some point it will be time to change. How will you know? When the digital ministry is no longer effectively accomplishing its function, it is time to change. When this time comes, your over-sight team will want to review the original mission, along with the technologies selected, and ask: if we were starting over right now, would we make the same decisions? Would our mission be the same? Most likely, some changes to the ministry will be needed at this point. It is possible that it will need to be com-pletely overhauled.

A Structured Foundation

This strategy framework may not work perfectly for all ministries. If you already have a digital ministry in place and have a strategy developed, then you may want to use this framework to ensure that you have covered all your bases. For others, this framework will offer a way to get started. In all cases, however, this framework provides a structured foundation for the development of a sound digital ministry.

7

Privacy and Security Considerations for Digital Ministry

If you really keep the royal law found in Scripture,
"Love your neighbor as yourself," you are doing right.

James 2:8

As you develop your ministry's digital strategy, it is important to consider how the use of digital tools can affect the privacy and security of those who use the tools, as well as the impact of these tools on your own ministry. Unlike previous generations, who stored everything in file cabinets and communicated via paper, we have to realize that every bit of information entered into a digital device can be easily logged, saved, copied and stolen. As a ministry, you must understand how your choices of digital tools can put your users and your ministry at risk and how you can mitigate those risks. This chapter will make you aware of many of these issues and discuss how your ministry could address them.

At this point, you may be asking yourself, "Do we really need to do anything? Shouldn't the users of technology already be aware of these issues? Isn't there always an inherent risk in visiting websites or using apps?" While these are good questions, I believe that we should be rising to a higher standard. To me, "loving your neighbor as yourself" should include taking every possible step to ensure the privacy and security of everyone who uses your ministry's digital tools.

According to a report in early 2012 from TRUSTe, an online privacy solutions provider, 90 percent of U.S. adults worry about their privacy online.[1] The report goes on to show that 95 percent of U.S. adults think that businesses have a responsibility to protect the online privacy of their customers. A February 2012 report by the Pew Internet & American Life Project found that many Americans are so concerned about privacy that they are "unfriending" people on Facebook at a high rate.[2] People care about privacy, and ministries should as well.

Know What Information You Have

To get started with privacy protection, first do an audit to understand just what information you have now or will be collecting once you have implemented your strategy. You probably will collect quite a bit more information about your users than you expect. Here are some types of information you may be collecting, intentionally or unintentionally, and the venues through which you may be collecting it.

Account information. If you ask the users of any of your systems (website, social media, mobile apps) to create an account with you, you are collecting and storing information about them. At a minimum, you are probably collecting their name and email address, and in many cases much, much more. If you are selling anything on your site or app, you are collecting payment information and possibly shipping information.

Forms. Does your website have a form people can fill out to be added to an email list? To update their directory information? To give their opinion in a survey? Any place on your website or in an app where a user enters information is a place where you are collecting information.

Social media. Using social media is a great way to create personal interactions with those you are trying to reach. When someone becomes your friend on Facebook, you have access to their personal information. When someone likes your page on Facebook or follows you on Twitter, you are granted access to information about them. When someone indicates that they will be attending your event on Facebook, you gain access to some of their profile information. In short, using social media also means that you now have access to quite a bit of personal information about those with whom you are interacting.

Automated data collection. Whenever anyone visits your website, they are transmitting information about themselves. Information such as their IP address, the type of computer they are using and even their network provider are available for you to capture if you so wish. Indeed, you probably *should* be capturing these data so that you can determine how well your website is being used and if you are meeting your goals. Analytics software (such as Google Analytics) and logging software are a part of good website management. The data they collect, however, are your responsibility.

If your ministry has created a mobile app, it will also be collecting information and possibly transmitting it back to you. Depending upon how it was designed, it may be collecting location information, information from the user's contact list and even her or his mobile phone number.

Develop a Privacy Policy

Once you have an understanding of the information that you are collecting, you can then make some decisions about what you will do with it. This is where the development of a privacy policy comes in. Most companies have these, but most ministries and churches do not.

The idea behind a privacy policy is to explain to anyone using your digital ministry tools exactly what information is being collected and what you will do with it. This policy should make users feel confident that their information is not going to be sold or given away to people or companies that they do not want to have it.

Users should be able to easily find the privacy policy on your website, and links to it should be available in appropriate places. It should be written in language that is easy to understand. An example of a good privacy policy is the one used by Biola University, shown in the sidebar.

BIOLA UNIVERSITY ONLINE PRIVACY POLICY STATEMENT

[Updated: January 24, 2012]

Biola University, Inc. (Biola) is committed to the responsible use of personal information collected from and about you while you are using the www.biola.edu website or any website or online service under the biola.edu domain name. Consistent with the California Online Privacy Protection Act of 2003, this privacy statement provides information about how this personal information may be used. Individual web pages under the biola.edu domain name may post additional privacy statements addressing more specific information collected on those pages.

Information We Collect

1. *Non-personally identifiable information*

As users access the website, Biola collects non-personally identifiable information such as IP address, browser type, and site usage. This information is *not* linked to any personal information and remains anonymous.

To collect this information, the university uses session "cookies" — that is, small text files that are placed on your computer's hard drive. The session cookies used by the university do *not* give us access to your computer and do *not* provide us with personally identifiable information. Session cookies are deleted when you close your browser. You may modify your browser settings to disallow cookies, but this may prevent you from taking full advantage of our website.

2. *Personally identifiable information*
Certain areas of our website collect voluntary information that is personally identifiable, such as name, zip code, and e-mail address. This is typically done through request and registration forms provided in order to learn of your interest in Biola and provide you with information and services.

Personally identifiable information may be collected as part of an online purchase, payment, or donation. In this case, Biola uses one of the following PCI-compliant third-party services to process your transaction. Prior to using these services, we encourage you to read the privacy policies listed below.

- FoxyCart.com LLC (non-student online payments and purchases) — http://www.foxycart.com/privacy -policy.html
- TouchNet Information Systems, Inc. (student account payments and non-student online payments and purchases) —http://www.touchnet.com/web/display/TN/ Privacy+Policy

- Vendini, Inc. (Biola Ticket Office purchases) — Select the Policies link at the bottom of each event's ticket sales page
- MBS Direct (online Biola Bookstore purchases) — http://www.mbsdirect.net/disclaimer.php

The university does *not* knowingly collect personally identifiable information from children (defined herein as minors younger than thirteen years of age) without obtaining parental consent. Implied parental consent includes, but is not limited to: use of parent login, use of parent-supplied credit card and inclusion of parent personal information on registration forms. Some Biola departments provide services to children. As a part of the online registration process for such services, we may request information such as a child's name, address, cell phone, email, gender, grade level, birth date, school attended, clothing size, church and ethnicity. This information is never sold or otherwise provided to third parties, although some information may be provided to other Biola departments in order to provide the child with information about Biola. Before registering online for a service, Biola requests that all children have their parents read this Privacy Policy as well as any additional Privacy Policy associated with the service for which they are registering, and that parents continue their involvement throughout the registration process.

Use of Information We Collect

1. *Use of non-personally identifiable information*
We use non-personally identifiable information while you are browsing the site to improve your individual experience and provide you with more individualized responses. We also ag-

gregate non-personally identifiable information from many users into statistical reports in order to better administer our website, diagnose server problems that may occur from time to time, and improve our website.

2. *Use of personally identifiable information*

By providing personally identifiable information, you imply consent to the collection and use of the information for the purposes for which it was provided. Your information is used to provide relevant materials, products and services you request, and to facilitate relationships with the University, such as the admissions process and fund raising programs. You may opt out of receiving information from Biola University by contacting the department from which the information came.

Only those Biola University employees who need personally identifiable information to perform a specific job are given access to the information. Unless required by law, personally identifiable information is only shared with third parties as necessary to provide the materials, products, and services you request. When third parties are given access to personally identifiable information, they are, by contract, not permitted to use or re-disclose any of the information for unauthorized purposes. Personally identifiable information is never sold to third parties.

Security

In order to protect the loss, misuse, or alteration of information gathered on our site, all information is stored within a controlled database environment accessible only to authorized University staff. However, as effective as any security measures implemented by the University may be, no security system is impenetrable. Biola University cannot guarantee the security of its database environment, nor can it guarantee that the information you provide will not be intercepted while being transmitted over the Internet.

Public Self-Disclosure

Biola University does not control the actions of its site visitors nor the use site visitors may make of publicly disclosed information. Please be aware that disclosing personally identifiable information on the site's bulletin boards, guest books, chat rooms or other such public forums may allow visitors to gather information and send unsolicited email. We encourage you to report any unsolicited/unwanted email or misuse of information to informationtechnology@biola.edu.

Links to Other Websites

Our website may include links to other websites outside the biola.edu domain, including co-branded or other affiliated sites that may or may not be owned or operated by Biola University. Such sites are not governed by this privacy statement. Users should become familiar with the privacy practices of those other sites.

Contact Information

Questions about this privacy policy should be directed to the University at informationtechnology@biola.edu.

Biola University
13800 Biola Avenue
La Mirada, CA 90639

The latest version of the Biola privacy policy is available at http://www.biola.edu/privacy. Used with permission.

Be Wise About the Information You Make Available

In addition to protecting the information you are collecting, you also need to protect the privacy of the information you are making public. Many times it is not appropriate to digitally provide information that your ministry originally made available in printed form or over the phone. Here are some examples of documents that might not be appropriate to offer in digital form.

Staff directories. Most organizations find it useful to have a listing of their staff members located somewhere on their website. This often includes the staff members' office phone numbers and email addresses. Although this provides a convenience to your constituents and makes your staff more accessible, you are also making that information available for spam mailing lists and telemarketer phone calls. If you do decide to list the email addresses on your website, it would be wise to also have a good spam filter on the staff members' emails.

Member directories. Many churches and ministries create directories of their members, listing the names, addresses and phone numbers of their members and families. While this is a great way to build community and provide convenience, making this available in a digital format can be problematic. The distribution of a paper-based directory can be controlled; that is, if one inadvertently falls into the hands of someone who should not have it, the damage is fairly limited. Making this directory available on the church website or a mobile app, however, can quickly lead to this information being harvested for marketing purposes or worse. If making your directory available online is an important aspect of your ministry, consider finding a solution that puts this directory behind some security mechanism, such as a login. You do not want to make this information publicly available.

Photographs and videos. Many individuals, for their own personal reasons, wish to keep photographs of themselves out of the public view. It may have to do with events in their past, legal issues or even just shyness. There also may be personal security reasons that someone does not want to be found online. For that reason, it can be problematic when people are unaware that their picture has been taken or that the ministry intends to place their pictures in a publicly accessible area online. On the other hand, in this day and age, in which almost everyone carries a high-quality camera in their pocket and security cameras are everywhere, most people should expect that their picture will be taken multiple times during the day whenever they are in public.

So how should a ministry handle this situation? My recommendation is to find a middle ground. One way to do this would be to only post high-quality, professional pictures or videos on your website or in your app. For these media, get permission and releases from the subjects to make it clear that they will be representing the ministry in a public way. For the more candid shots (like at a church picnic, concert or other ministry event), I would recommend relying on personal pictures and videos taken by those in attendance who can then share them via their own Facebook or photo-sharing page. If this is not an alternative that will work for your ministry and you would like to post these images and videos on your own site or Facebook page, then be sure you make it clear that you are doing so. Provide a method for those who do not want their images posted online to let you know. You should also provide a way for people to easily notify you if you posted something that they want taken down.

Finally, a quick word about posting images of children: for any pictures or videos of children posted on the ministry website or Facebook page or included in an app, guardians must grant permission. With all the concern about child custody issues, abductions and abuse, there is no excuse for a ministry not doing everything it can to protect children.

News about missionaries. I want to include some specific guidance about posting information about and photographs of missionaries. Many ministries support missionaries, and the Internet is a great way to provide the latest news about them and information about how to support them. Many missionaries, however, are working in countries that are closed or even hostile to Christianity. In those cases, posting information and pictures about them could jeopardize their ministry or even their physical safety. I would suggest getting specific permission from each missionary before posting their information digitally. Missionaries frequently have specific policies about what information can be made public and what information cannot.

Mass emails. When sending emails to your constituents, you should take precautions to be sure that you are not inadvertently sharing all the email addresses. There is no excuse for a ministry to send out an email to dozens or hundreds of people and have all the emails addresses show up in the email. Those emails are likely to show up on a spammer's list within weeks!

I can recommend a couple of ways to ensure that you are protecting these email addresses. First, you can use an email management application, such as Constant Contact. Services such as this not only can protect email addresses but also will provide tools to help you manage email campaigns. If you do not need (or cannot afford to pay for) an email management application, then the simple answer is to never put email addresses in the "to" or "cc" (carbon copy) fields when sending a mass email. Leave those fields blank and put all of your email addresses in the "bcc" (blind carbon copy) field. If your email tool does not allow a blank "to" field, then put your own ministry's email address in this field.

Prayer requests. Many churches and ministries want to provide prayer support for their members via a website or app. This can be a wonderful use of digital technologies, but if you want to do this, you should also proceed with caution. It should be extremely clear to the user exactly what will happen with the information posted in the prayer request. Will it be sent around in an email? Will it be posted back to a website or an app? It is essential that a ministry protects any private information posted in a prayer request.

Comments. Finally, I would like to address the monitoring of comments. If your ministry has any sort of interactive forum, discussion board, Facebook page or any other venue through which users can post their own ideas or comments, it is essential to monitor those comments to ensure the safety of your users' information. Most of the time, we think of monitoring comments in order to remove offensive or slanderous statements. But we should also be sure that we monitor comments in case someone posts something that reveals information about themselves (or someone else) they may not want to be public. In many cases, people who post comments do so out of emotion and may not understand the implications of what they are posting. This especially goes for posting to sites like Facebook, where a large number of people may see the post.

For example, a member of the church youth group could be upset with someone else in the group and post, "J. D. really sucks. Call him up and tell him so at 555-1212." Another example might be more innocent, as if someone would post, "My family is leaving for a three-week trip to Europe tomorrow, I am so excited! I have to leave my new iPad at home, hope it is safe! LOL." These examples may be a bit exaggerated, but can you see the problem here? Your ministry does not want to be liable for allowing comments such as these to linger on your website or Facebook page for very long.

Security Concerns for Digital Ministry

Closely related to concerns over privacy of the information you are storing are the issues related to the protection of your ministry. The use of digital tools does create some risks, and you should be sure that you are taking steps to protect yourself and the information you are disseminating. Some guidance on managing security concerns follows.

Respecting intellectual property. It is important that your ministry respect intellectual property laws. All content on your site,

Facebook page or app should be the property of your ministry. Period. All pictures, music, videos and text should be created, licensed or owned by your ministry. This includes worship music! Most music is copyrighted and requires payment of a special license fee to use it online (above and beyond what you pay to use it in a worship service). This also goes for background music in videos: if you do not have a license to use it, don't. But what if you do not know if you have the rights to something? My simple rule of thumb here is: if you do not know if you are allowed to put something on your website, don't.

Providing wireless Internet access. Many churches or ministries have facilities in which they could provide wireless Internet access (Wi-Fi). Doing this provides a service to those attending a service or using the facility and, in fact, may be an essential part of what your ministry does. You should carefully consider exactly how you want to provide this access, however, before doing so.

One of the first issues to consider is whether or not your wireless access should be available via an open network. An open network is simply a network that does not require a password in order to use it. Providing access via an open network greatly simplifies things and allows anyone to bring their device and get on the network quickly. Providing access in this way can, however, cause some problems. First, you will not have any control over who is on your network. Wireless signals can be read up to two or even three hundred feet away and, with special equipment, someone may be able to access your signal from miles away. If you provide Wi-Fi access with no login, you will have to be comfortable not knowing who is on your network and for what purpose. If you are located near businesses or residential neighborhoods, you could potentially have dozens of people using your signal (and thus slowing it down) every day.

Another reason to not have an open network is the possibility of someone snooping on your network, accessing unsecured computers or even "tapping" the traffic on your network. Someone could potentially intercept account numbers or passwords by simply connecting a network analysis device to this open network and reading the information being transferred.

For these reasons, I highly recommend that most ministries *not* offer open Wi-Fi access at their facilities. If offering an open network is essential for your ministry, then I suggest providing two options: a secured network for your regular users that requires a password, and an open network for guests, which has limited bandwidth, displays warnings about its use and logs people off after a limited time.

Using a web content filter. If you are providing Internet access to your employees, visitors or anyone else, the question of filtering content has probably come up. Allowing your employees, members and guests unfiltered access to the Internet could potentially lead to many problems. You do not want your employees accessing sites that are not consistent with your mission. You do not want a visitor using your Internet to look at pornography online.

Several options for web content filtering are available to you. I suggest working with a company that provides software that allows you to set the filter to your liking and that provides you with support. If you cannot afford this sort of solution, another simple solution is to use a free DNS-based filter, such as that provided by OpenDNS.

Backing up data. You may be asking, "How is backup related to security?" Well, consider this: if someone decided they did not want your ministry to succeed and was able to not just bring down your server but also destroy all of your data, would you be able to continue as a ministry? Would it affect your ability to communicate? Get donations?

Every ministry should back up all of its data: the data on each of the devices it uses and the data on its servers. My suggestion is to back up your data automatically at least once a week, if not more often. Do not rely on your employees to back up their own data;

there should be an automated process that does it for them. As for the servers: work with your hosting company to be sure that the data are being backed up and made available to you. If you use services such as Google Docs or Web-based email, you should also make a copy of the data on these sites as well. What if, for whatever reason, Google or your email cannot be reached or goes down? What if you forget your password or someone maliciously changes it? You should have your own copy of these data.

When you are backing up your data, be sure that one copy of the backup is stored offsite. A catastrophe such as a fire, tornado or earthquake could mean the loss of your data. If you keep copies of your backed-up data at the same location as the originals of the data, then in events such as these, you risk losing your backups as well. If you are using some sort of Internet-based backup, it is essential to understand how this backup service is storing your data. Make sure this service is not in the same location as you are so that it is not subject to the same catastrophes. If a tornado takes you out, you don't want it to take out your backup too!

Writing policies for ministry employees and volunteers. Your staff, volunteers and even those who come into your facilities all have access to your information. One important way to keep your digital ministry safe is to have effective policies for those who regularly access your information. These folks can, inadvertently, damage the ministry by being careless in their use of the Internet or apps or by sharing information with those wishing to harm the ministry. It is essential that your employees, volunteers and anyone who accesses ministry information follow these simple rules.

- *Always keep the operating system and antivirus software up to date.* This is a simple procedure that will ensure that the majority of malware is not loaded onto your network. Most of the time, this updating can be automated.

- *Only post financial and account information on secure websites.* When it is necessary to use account numbers and logins that are part of the ministry, be sure that the website that you are using is secured with encryption. You can tell if a website is secure by the use of the "https" protocol, which should be visible in the address bar.

- *Never respond to an unsolicited email.* If an employee receives an unsolicited email from the ministry's bank or credit card company that asks them to provide some information, this is likely a scheme to get them to share financial information so that the account can be stolen. Don't do it.

- *Never give away any information about the ministry to anyone—whether online, over the phone or in person.* Similar to the previous point: if someone calls you or even asks in person for the ministry's financial information, do not give it away. This also holds true for the personal information of those who work there or are served by the ministry.

- *Do not store any ministry-related financial account information on a digital device.* This is a bit more difficult. When you enter credit card information, user account information and passwords, most browsers offer to remember or save that information for future use. If the device is sometimes used by someone who is not authorized to make purchases with those accounts or log in to those servers, however, you do not want the computer to have that information available.

- *All passwords used for ministry purposes should be complex.* Related to the above point is this one: it should be nearly impossible for someone to guess a password that is essential to the ministry. A complex password is one that: (a) is not a term found in the dictionary; (b) contains upper- and lowercase letters; (c) contains at least one number; (d) contains at least one "special character," such as an exclamation point; and (e) is at least eight characters long. A password that meets all of these criteria can be difficult to remember, but I suggest that you require that employees have passwords that meet at least *some* of these criteria. Then if someone does come into the possession of a device that can access ministry resources, he or she will not be able to guess the password. One simple way to create this kind of password is to have each character in the password be the first letter in a phrase, such as "JC1mLaS!" for "Jesus Christ is my Lord and Savior!" (with a "1" replacing the "i").

- *Never access ministry information over an open wireless network.* If an employee is doing work at a coffee shop or a hotel or similar place, chances are that they are on an open wireless network. Information sent over an open network can be "listened" to and intercepted. A good policy is to never allow access to ministry resources (or your own personal information) over any network that allows anyone to use it without a password.

- *Never leave a mobile device unattended.* If your ministry has employees who travel frequently, be sure they understand that one of the primary ways that thieves steal organizational information is by simply stealing the devices themselves. Never leave a mobile device unattended! If employees travel frequently and the risk to your ministry is high if information is stolen, consider taking additional steps, such as encrypting the hard drive.

Of course, these suggested policies are relevant at the time of this writing. As we move into an even more mobile and digital age, these policies may need to be modified. Websites such as staysafe online.org are a good resource for this.

Securing your server. In addition to making sure your employees are doing their part to keep ministry information safe, it is also important to ensure that any information stored on a ministry server is safe. Whether you host your own server at your ministry or you work with a provider, securing your online data should be a top priority. One of the best ways you can do this is by making sure that your server has a digital certificate, which encrypts all communication that your server makes over the Internet. You should also ensure that your server has an up-to-date operating system and is behind a firewall. If you host the server yourself, then this is your responsibility. If you work with a provider, then you will want to ensure that they take care of all of this.

Hiring a white hat. No, this is not about fashion attire! This final suggestion is simple: to be sure your ministry is securing its information in the best way possible, you can hire someone to try to break in. There are people, called "white-hat hackers," who do this for a living. You can ask them to try to break into your server, monitor your wireless network or even get employees to reveal information over the phone. Doing this may seem extreme, but your information is one of your most valuable commodities. So why not put your security measures to the test?

Just the Tip of the Iceberg

In this chapter, I have provided some basic guidelines for developing a digital ministry that respects the privacy of its constituents and protects its information. To me, this is simply being a good steward of the resources God has given us. The steps outlined in this chapter are just a starting point for your ministry. I highly recommend that privacy and security considerations be written directly into your ministry's digital strategy and reviewed on a regular basis. I hope this chapter is helpful in getting you started down this path.

Conclusion

"His master replied, 'Well done, good and faithful servant! You have been faithful with a few things; I will put you in charge of many things. Come and share your master's happiness!'"

Matthew 25:23

As you move forward with your digital ministry, I pray that the resources and guidance that this book provides will help you to be successful in reaching your goals. As you look to the future, let me encourage you with a few closing thoughts that summarize much of what I have been trying to communicate in the previous seven chapters.

Recognize that God Has Given Us These Tools

In the first chapter, I shared with you how God has used different technologies as tools to bring about his plans. Through the centuries, Christians have recognized this and have used these tools boldly. I do not believe it was an accident that the dot-com bubble of the early 2000s led to a wired world. And I believe that we are called to recognize this strategic moment in time and to use these tools to move forward.

Build Relationships

At every step in the process as you are developing your strategy, the idea of building relationships should be in the forefront of your mind. Do not think of digital tools as simply a way to do something more efficiently or to let more people know about your ministry. While this is true, if this is all you are doing with your digital ministry, it will be obvious to your users. Instead, engage with them on a more personal level, sharing a bit of yourself and your ministry with them. Powerful tools such as social media and mobile devices are very personal and are frequently helpful in engaging with constituents in more intimate ways.

Work Strategically

If you learned anything from this book, it should be this: in order to be successful in the long term, you must work strategically. In the last part of this book, we reviewed exactly what it means to have a strategy and the steps you can take to develop one. I encourage you to be sure you work through all the steps. It is human nature to want to skip the steps that require the most effort: researching, identifying the processes and writing everything down. Take the time to do all the steps; it will be well worth it in the end.

Lord, I ask that you bless the readers of this book and the ministries in which they are involved. Give them wisdom and discipline as they work through the decisions necessary to develop strategies for their digital ministry. I pray that you would bless the ministries with the resources they need in order to fulfill their missions and to reach the world for you. Amen.

Appendix A

Digital Tool Categories

Following is a list of the primary categories of digital tools at the time of this writing. This is by no means a complete listing, but you can use it to get started thinking about some of the ways you might incorporate digital technologies in your ministry.

Blog

A blog (short for *web-log*) is a website centered on short- to medium-length articles and videos and photos. An individual or a group can author these articles, with the latest article appearing on top. A blog is generally used to provide opinions or inspirational messages on a regular basis. Blogging software is generally very easy to use and provides a simple interface for posting to the blog. Blogging software can also be the basis for an entire website, which is a good fit if the blog is going to be the primary content around which the site is centered.

A good example of a ministry blog would be something like ChurchMarketingSucks.com, which has the latest article on the front page and links to other articles. You can get started blogging for free at wordpress.com or blogger.com. If you want to do more than blogging, using a content management system will be the best direction to go.

Microblog

A microblog is a place to post quick status updates or links to stories or photos. Twitter and Tumblr are examples of microblogs, although even Facebook status updates could be considered a form of microblogging. Microblogging includes a form of social networking, in that you "follow" the posts of microbloggers. Unlike on social networks, however, the person you are following does not have to follow you back. Your ministry could have a microblog, or you could opt to make it more personal by doing your ministry microblogging using your own personal account.

A good example of microblogging for ministry purposes is the Twitter account DesiringGod. Microblogging does not cost anything but the time you put into it.

Podcast

A podcast is a series of audio recordings (and now more frequently video, though those can be called *vidcasts* or *videocasts*) that are available over the Internet. Getting their name from the iPod, podcasts are audio and video files that users can subscribe to through iTunes or other "podcatchers" and receive the new recordings as soon as they are posted. Podcasts could be used for distributing a radio-type show over the Internet or as a way for church members to keep up with weekly sermons.

An example of a ministry podcast would be those at LifeChurch.tv, where they podcast the audio and video of their weekly service. See rss.lifechurch.tv/archive.php for a listing of their latest podcasts.

Email Campaign

The idea of an email campaign is to send regular email messages to a list of subscribers to keep them informed about your ministry. Software for managing an email campaign generally includes ways for people to subscribe to your mailing list and unsubscribe. The software will manage your mailing lists and help you generate your email. It will also track who opens the email and give statistics on whether they click any of the links in the email. Constant Contact and MailChimp are two examples of software in this category.

Content Management Systems

A content management system (CMS) is a software package designed to manage a medium-to-complex website that contains many different types of information (content). This software separates the complexity of website management from the creation and posting of content such as videos, discussion boards, articles, slideshows, blog posts and social media integration. A CMS is not as simple to install, set up and use as a blog, but its capabilities are much more comprehensive. Some of the more popular content management software tools are wordpress.org, joomla.org and drupal.org.

Church Management Systems

A special subset of content management software, called a *church management system*, deserves special attention. This software provides specialized content management for churches, including pages for staff, sermons, donations and pages for specific ministries that are already set up. This software also may include features to manage attendance and mailing lists. There is a wide range of church management system providers, from the inexpensive Web-Empowered Church (webempoweredchurch.org) to the full-featured software offered by Monk Development (monkdevelopment.com).

Short Message Service (SMS)

SMS, or text messaging, can be used as a way to communicate directly to the mobile phones of those in your ministry. This can be an effective way to coordinate for events or simply encourage those who subscribe. For sending to a small number of people, you can simply use your phone; for larger groups or more structured campaigns, you will want to use a service such as ohdontforget.com or trumpia.com.

Another way to do an SMS campaign is through SMS response. In this case, you have people text-message you with a request for more information, and then you reply with a link or email address. You may want to purchase a "short code" SMS number, which is a five- or six-digit number to which people can send a text. Trumpia.com also provides this service.

Social Network

A social network is a website where users can interact and share messages, photos, videos and links and even play games with one another. Users give each other permission to interact by identifying them as "friends." The social network category is quite broad and, really, there is only one relevant player right now: Facebook. Do not build your own social network unless there is truly something unique that you can offer that Facebook does not. Ning.com is an example of a tool that allows you to create your own social network.

Mobile App

A mobile app is simply a software application designed to run on a mobile device. Mobile apps can be designed to specifically take advantage of the mobile device's capabilities, such as GPS, text-messaging and the ability to make a phone call. The difference between mobile apps and mobile-friendly websites was discussed in chapter 2. Creating a mobile app is not easy and generally will require the work of a consulting service.

Photo and Video Sharing

Photo- and video-sharing services allow anyone to upload a picture or a video and instantly make it available. As more and more people have high-quality cameras on their mobile devices, the popularity of this service is increasing rapidly. Many of these services integrate directly with social media sites such as Facebook or Twitter, allowing near real-time access. Some of the most popular of these services include Flickr, Instagram and YouTube. Ministries can use these types of services to share photos or videos of events or to highlight a recent news story.

Appendix B

Research Report

BEST PRACTICES IN INTERNET MINISTRY

Released November 7, 2008

David T. Bourgeois, PhD

Introduction

For the past two years, I have been conducting research on Internet ministry. This has included one-on-one interviews with leaders in the field, case studies, the development of my own church's website and the implementation of a survey taken by over three hundred different ministry organizations. This culminated last month in the presentation of the findings of my research as a keynote at the Internet Ministry Conference in Grand Rapids, Michigan. The focus of the presentation was on the best practices of Internet ministry.

How does one determine best practices? My approach was to survey ministry organizations on how they implemented and maintained their Internet ministry, as well as to ask questions that let me determine how successful they viewed their ministry to be. By then selecting the organizations that viewed their ministries as extremely successful, I could look for commonalities in how they answered the other questions. But what types of questions should be asked?

Digital Ministry Framework

As a researcher and professor in the information systems field, I have come to understand that the most difficult part of creating or implementing any system is not the technology; it is the people and processes involved that require the most effort. The *digital ministry framework* embodies all three aspects of implementing an Internet ministry: technology, people and process. This is an important definition because many, many organizations looking to start an online ministry immediately focus on the technology and completely ignore the more difficult decisions surrounding the people involved and the processes undertaken to implement and maintain the ministry. None of the three components are any more important than the other: all three play an equal role in supporting a successful Internet ministry.

Demographics

Representatives from 344 organizations took this survey, which was available online from November 2007 to April 2008. The majority of the organizations represented in this survey could be classified as small ministries that have little resources available to devote to the Internet. A short breakdown of the demographics follows.

- 68 percent were churches; the other 32 percent were broken down between organizations focused on discipleship, evangelism and education.

- 77 percent had twenty-five or fewer people on staff.

- 53 percent spent less than $1,000 per year on their web ministry.

- 69 percent spent less than ten hours per week working on their website.

Success

As explained above, several questions on the survey were directed toward understanding if the members of the organization considered their Internet ministry successful. Depending upon how they answered these questions, a "success score" was developed and allowed me to then compare the answers of other questions to the success. But overall, how successful do these organizations feel their Internet ministry is? The answers were not very encouraging.

- Only 36 percent of the respondents thought their Internet ministry was successful.

- For churches only, the answer dropped to 33 percent that considered their digital ministry a success.

- Organization size did not seem to affect the success score, as organizations with only one staff member had higher average success (47 percent) than larger organizations, though not as high as those with over twenty-five on staff (49 percent success):

  - 47 percent of organizations with a staff size of one reported success.

  - 34 percent of organizations with a staff size of two to five reported success.

  - 29 percent of organizations with a staff size of six to twenty-five reported success.

  - 49 percent of organizations with a staff size of more than twenty-five reported success.

- Money did play a role. As budget sizes increased, so did success. However, a large majority of organizations taking the survey had budgets under $1,000.

  - 25 percent of organizations with an annual budget less than $500 reported success.

- 30 percent of organizations with an annual budget of $500 to $1,000 reported success.

- 36 percent of organizations with an annual budget of $1,000 to $10,000 reported success.

- 64 percent of organizations with an annual budget more than $10,000 reported success.

- The amount of time spent on the site did play a role as well, with higher success scores as the amount of time spent on the site increased. Again, though, 69 percent of the organizations reported spending less than ten hours per week.

  - 24 percent of organizations that spent less than ten hours per week reported success.

  - 57 percent of organizations that spent ten to twenty hours per week reported success.

  - 71 percent of organizations that spent twenty to forty hours per week reported success.

  - 73 percent of organizations that spent more than forty hours per week reported success.

We can see from the above results that having more money to spend on Internet ministry and devoting more time to it brings about increased success. This should come as no surprise. Many smaller organizations were still able to implement successful web ministries, however, while having smaller budgets and limited time. What did these organizations have in common? What can we learn from these organizations?

Findings

As stated earlier, the survey asked questions in the three components of the digital ministry framework: technology, people and process. The findings will be categorized under those three categories as well.

Technology

The technology component of Internet ministry includes not just what server platform and web software are used, but also the decisions surrounding what features should go on the website (podcasts, blogs, videos, etc.), how much to integrate the ministry with existing sites (such as social networks, blogs and photo sharing), data collection and search engine optimization. The survey asked several questions in this area.

- Was the Internet technology used purchased from an outside organization or was it built internally? Those that indicated that they purchased their software reported success 36 percent of the time; those that indicated that they built it reported success 41 percent of the time.

- What features were included in the Internet ministry? Those that included more interactive features (such as blogs and videos) reported much greater success than those that did not.

  - Organizations that included announcements had a success rate 2 percent higher than those that did not.

  - Organizations that included a calendar had a success rate 4 percent higher than those that did not.

  - Organizations that included blogs had a success rate 19 percent higher than those that did not.

  - Organizations that included podcasts had a success rate 15 percent higher than those that did not.

  - Organizations that included videos had a success rate 22 percent higher than those that did not.

- What other websites did you integrate with? Organizations that included integration with social media sites reported much greater success than those that did not.

- Organizations that integrated with blog sites reported slightly higher success rates than those that did not (Blogger: 1 percent higher; Wordpress: 5 percent higher).

- Organizations that integrated with photo-sharing sites reported much higher success rates than those that did not (Photobucket: 15 percent higher; Flickr: 45 percent higher).

- Organizations that integrated with video-sharing sites reported much higher success rates than those that did not (YouTube: 25 percent higher; GodTube: 23 percent higher).

- Organizations that integrated with social networking sites reported much higher success rates than those that did not (Facebook: 24 percent higher; MySpace: 22 percent higher).

- Organizations that collected data about their sites (via tools such as Google Analytics) were much more successful than those that did not. *This finding is one of the largest differences between those who reported success and those who did not.*

  - Organizations collecting data about their site reported success 51 percent of the time.

  - Organizations not collecting data about their site reported success 16 percent of the time.

- Organizations that had done some form of search engine optimization (SEO) were more successful than those that had not.

  - Organizations that did SEO reported success 51 percent of the time.

  - Organizations that did not do SEO reported success 25 percent of the time.

People

The people component of the framework incorporates all the individuals who are a part of your ministry and how they are used as part of the Internet presence you are developing. Who is ultimately responsible for the website—and is it in their job description? Who is going to update the website? Who sets the direction for the website? Who is going to build the site—do you have the ability to do this in-house or should an outside consultant be brought in? And finally: what about using volunteers for your web ministry?

- Is there one person who is responsible for the website? Forty-nine percent of organizations who had one person responsible for the site reported success, compared to 22 percent of those who did not have one responsible person.

- Is there a group of people who meet regularly to set direction for the website? Fifty-two percent of organizations who had such a team reported success, compared to 31 percent of those who did not have a team.

- Who gave input into the features that went into the website?

  - Organizations that had volunteers give input into the features on the website reported success 5 percent *less often* than those that did not.

  - Organizations that had staff give input into the features on the website reported success 5 percent *less often* than those that did not.

  - Organizations that had leadership give input into the features on the website reported success 6 percent more often than those that did not.

  - Organizations that had an outside consultant give input into the features on the website reported success 10 percent more often than those that did not.

- Who built the website? Did you use volunteers, internal staff, outside consultants or licensed software from a vendor?

- Organizations that had volunteers build the website reported success 16 percent *less often* than those that did not.

- Organizations that licensed their website from a vendor/provider reported success 3 percent more often than those that did not.

- Organizations that used outside consultants to build their website reported success 6 percent more often than those that did not.

- Organizations that utilized their internal IT staff to build their website reported success 9 percent more often than those that did not.

As you can see from the last two questions, the use of volunteers seems to have quite a negative impact on the success of Internet ministry. Many ministry organizations, however, have no choice but to rely on volunteers. An open-ended question on the survey that asked for more feedback on the use of volunteers also trended negative: it seems that relying on volunteers to be an integral part of creating or maintaining a web ministry does not work out well. However, in several of the case studies I have done as a follow-up to this research, I found that many organizations have found success with volunteers doing less mission-critical tasks, such as moderating forums or one-time content creation projects.

Process

The *process* component of the digital ministry framework involves defining the steps the organization will take to implement and maintain the Internet ministry. This includes the planning process: creating goals for the online ministry and researching its needs. It also includes the process for maintaining the site once it is up and running. Here are the results from some of the key questions.

- Did you have any written goals or a mission statement for your Internet ministry? Forty-five percent of organizations that answered "yes" reported success, compared to 30 percent success for those that reported "no."

- Did you develop a profile of your target user? Forty-six percent of organizations that answered "yes" reported success, compared to 28 percent success for those that reported "no."

- Did you collect any data or do any research in preparation for developing your web ministry? Fifty-two percent of organizations that answered "yes" reported success, compared to 26 percent success for those that reported "no."

- Did you provide any training on your web ministry? Forty-two percent of organizations that answered "yes" reported success, compared to 32 percent success for those that reported "no."

- Do you have a centralized approval process? Forty-three percent of organizations that answered "yes" reported success, compared to 35 percent success for those that reported "no."

- Do you allow ministries to directly update their own related pages? Forty-four percent of organizations that answered "yes" reported success, compared to 30 percent success for those that reported "no."

Best Practices

After reviewing the above findings, I identified several organizations that, according to their survey responses, were extremely successful at their Internet ministry. I talked with several respondents about how they implemented their ministries and specifically followed up on many of the questions listed in the findings above. This gave me a more in-depth understanding of how these findings could be put in context. By combining the survey data with the case studies, I have developed a set of twelve best practices that I believe will help ministries be more successful using the Internet. These are summarized below.

Technology

1. The specific software you use is not as important as content. While a nice-looking site is important, it is the content that provides the value to the users.

2. Use interactive content such as blogs, podcasts and videos as much as possible.

3. Do not build new features yourself if you can integrate existing sites that do the same thing. For example: put your videos on YouTube and integrate them into your site instead of hosting the videos yourself.

4. Install data-collection code on your site and analyze it!

People

5. Recognize your limits. Get outside help if you need it!

6. Use volunteers wisely, sparingly.

7. Have a team responsible for setting direction.

8. Designate one person to be ultimately responsible for the site.

Process

9. Planning may be the most important step in the implementation of an Internet ministry.

10. Develop written goals and/or a mission statement to guide you. Refer to these as you make decisions about features and technologies for your ministry.

11. Have a centralized approval process for site updating.

12. Allow for distributed updating of information that belongs to different parts of your ministry.

I realize that not all of these best practices will make sense for every organization. These are meant as general guidelines that will assist ministries in developing the most successful Internet ministry possible. These best practices are skewed toward smaller organizations that have limited resources. As we saw when reviewing the success data, organizations that can spend money and devote a lot of time to their Internet ministries will be more successful.

Below is the Internet ministry survey used to develop the best practices report. It was posted to the gospel.com website from November 2007 through April 2008. Over three hundred individuals responded to the survey.

Internet Ministry Survey

Demographics

1. What best describes the primary activity of your organization?

    ___ church

    ___ discipleship

    ___ evangelism

    ___ education

    ___ other: _____

2. What is the size of your staff?

    ___ 1

    ___ 2 to 5

    ___ 6 to 25

    ___ 26 to 100

    ___ more than 100

3. Is your organization location-specific? (In other words, are you primarily serving a specific geographic community?)

    ___ yes

    ___ no

4. What do you annually spend on your website, including hosting, administration, staff, design and any other services?

___ <$500 (USD)

___ $500 - $1,000

___ $1,000 - $10,000

___ $10,000 - $50,000

___ $50,000 - $100,000

___ >$100,000

5. The money spent on your website is approximately what percent of your overall organization budget?

___ <1%

___ 1-5%

___ 6-10%

___ 11-25%

___ 26-50%

___ >50%

6. How many total hours a week (on average) are spent by your staff maintaining, developing or producing content for your website?

___ <10

___ 11-20

___ 21-40

___ >40

7. Is there one person on staff whose job description makes her or him fully responsible for the website?

___ yes

___ no

8. Does your organization have a team of people that regularly meets specifically to set the direction of the website?

___ yes

___ no

Implementation

The following questions relate to the process of the design, development and implementation of your current website.

9. During the planning stages of your website, did you create written goals and/or a mission statement?

___ yes

___ no

10. During the planning stages of your website, did you collect any data to help plan which features should be in your website (for example, surveys or focus groups)?

    ___ yes

    ___ no

11. During the planning stages of your website, did you develop a profile of your target user?

    ___ yes

    ___ no

12. Which stakeholders gave significant input into the feature set of your website? (Check all that apply.)

    ___ leadership

    ___ staff

    ___ volunteers

    ___ outside consultant

    ___ other: _____

    ___ none

13. The decision making for the website implementation was made by:

    ___ one person

    ___ a team of people

14. How was your website built? (Check all that apply.)

    ___ internal staff/IT

    ___ volunteers

    ___ licensing a vendor-supplied website (for example, Church Community Builder)

    ___ outside contractor/consultant

15. Did you provide any training on the use of your website to your organization?

    ___ yes

    ___ no

Characteristics of Website

16. Is your website primarily intended for use by those already a part of your organization?

___ yes

___ no

17. Which of the following describes features that are available on your website? (Check all that apply.)

___ internal use

___ donations

___ membership

___ communication

___ education

___ volunteer recruitment

___ relationship building

18. Of the following list of features, mark which ones you have and which ones have been updated in the past seven days.

announcements	___ have this	___ updated in last 7 days
calendar	___ have this	___ updated in last 7 days
blog	___ have this	___ updated in last 7 days
podcast/audio	___ have this	___ updated in last 7 days
vidcast/videos	___ have this	___ updated in last 7 days
pictures	___ have this	___ updated in last 7 days

19. Do you require an approval process before updates are made to your website?

___ yes

___ no

20. Do you allow different groups/ministries within your organization to directly update their associated webpages?

___ yes

___ no

___ n/a

Marketing

21. Which of the following websites, if any, do you utilize as part of

your ministry? (Check all that apply.)

___ Facebook

___ MySpace

___ SecondLife

___ YouTube

___ Photobucket

___ Flickr

___ MyChurch

___ GodTube

___ BibleGateway

___ Blogger

___ WordPress

___ Mailing lists/groups such as Yahoo! groups

___ others (please list): _____

22. Have you done any search engine optimization work on your website?

___ yes

___ no

23. Are you satisfied with where your site ranks on search engine results?

___ yes

___ no

___ never tried it/not important

24. What is the primary means for your target users to find your website? (Select one.)

___ search engine results

___ link in email message

___ link from other sites

___ paid advertisements

___ printed materials

___ word of mouth

___ other: _____

Success of Website

Select the answer that best describes your agreement with the following statements.

25. We are collecting data that measure how our website is being used.

    1 (Strongly disagree) 2 3 4 5 6 (Strongly agree)

26. I would recommend my organization's website as a model for others to follow.

    1 (Strongly disagree) 2 3 4 5 6 (Strongly agree)

27. If I had the budget, I would make significant changes to our website.

    1 (Strongly disagree) 2 3 4 5 6 (Strongly agree)

28. Our website is fully integrated into every aspect of our ministry.

    1 (Strongly disagree) 2 3 4 5 6 (Strongly agree)

29. Our website has made a huge impact on our ministry.

    1 (Strongly disagree) 2 3 4 5 6 (Strongly agree)

Closing Questions (open-ended)

30. What has been your experience using volunteers to help with your website?

31. Relate the one key factor that you feel has contributed to the successful completion of your website implementation.

32. Please elaborate on any question you would like to answer further, or provide any additional comments that would help us.

33. This research project is being used to develop materials for Internet ministry. Would you be willing to make your organization available for further research?

    ___ yes

    ___ no

    If yes, please give contact information.

       email:

       web address:

       phone number:

       contact name:

    Please note: not all organizations will be contacted.

This report, the survey and all data collected as part of this project were created by David Bourgeois, PhD. You may use this survey for your own use, but please give credit to David Bourgeois.

Appendix C

Church Web Usage Survey

In 2007, I conducted a survey of the congregation of my church, as part of the research step of our website redesign. The following survey was printed out on the front and back of an 8½" x 5½" sheet of paper and inserted into our church bulletin.

Note: "The Passage," "WOW" and "WC" represent large ministries within our church.

As part of an effort to make more effective use of the Internet, we need to understand how you use it. Please fill this out and turn in it as directed or directly to the church office. *Please only fill this survey out once!*

Age:	Gender: Male Female	I am in a leadership position at this church.

Church group(s) I am a part of:

    Junior High   High School   The Passage   WOW   WC

    Adult Sunday School class (enter name): _____

    Other small group(s) (enter name/description): _____

Activity	How often I usually do this...				
	More than once a day	Once a day	A few times a week	Once a week or less	I don't do this
I use a computer.					
I check my email.					
I visit websites.					
I send or receive an instant message (IM).					
I use text messaging on my cell phone.					

I have done the following on the Internet in the last month (check all that apply):

Read news/sports/weather stories	Searched for information
Purchased something	Online banking
Viewed maps/got driving directions	Listened to a podcast
Visited a social network site (MySpace, Friendster, etc.)	Updated my social network profile
Viewed pictures of family/friends	Uploaded pictures to share
Watched a video	Uploaded a video
Read a blog	Wrote a blog entry

If your pastor or group leader had a blog or website they updated once or more a week, would you read it?	Yes	No
If the church made registration for events available online, would you use it?	Yes	No
If the church made it possible to do regular giving online, would you do it?	Yes	No

How important is a church website?

    Very important   Important   Somewhat important   Not important

What are your three favorite websites?

What sorts of features would you like to see on our church website?

Please feel free to leave any other comments below.

Figure C.1.

Notes

Introduction

[1]Shane Hipps, conversation with author, January 28, 2009.

[2]"KONY 2012," YouTube, accessed August 2, 2012, <www.youtube.com/watch?v=Y4MnpzG5Sqc>.

[3]"KONY 2012: Success or Failure?" *International Broadcasting Trust*, accessed August 6, 2012, <www.ibt.org.uk/all_documents/research/IBT_KonySOweb.pdf>.

[4]*The Internet Encyclopedia*, vol. 1, ed. Hossein Bidgoli (New York: Wiley, 2003), s.v. "Global Diffusion of the Internet," p. 38; "Internet Users in the World," Internet World Stats: Usage and Population Statistics," <www.internetworldstats.com/stats.htm>.

[5]Key Facts, Facebook newsroom, accessed October 12, 2012, <www.facebook.com/content/default.aspx?NewsAreaID=22>; Statistics, YouTube, accessed October 12, 2012, <www.youtube.com/t/press_statistics>.

1 What Hath God Wrought?

[1]Thomas Friedman, "The World Is Flat," MIT Video, 1:15:13. May 16, 2005, <http://video.mit.edu/watch/the-world-is-flat-9145/>.

[2]Michael Green, *Evangelism in the Early Church* (Grand Rapids: Eerdmans, 1970), p. 16.

[3]T. C. Skeat, "The Origin of the Christian Codex," *Zeitschrift für Papyrologie und Epigraphik*, Bd. 102 (1994): 263-68.

[4]For more insight into the impact of the telegraph, see Tom Standage, *The Victorian Internet: The Remarkable Story of the Telegraph and the Nineteenth Century's On-line Pioneers* (New York: Walker and Company, 2007).

[5]Charles Frederick Briggs and Augustus Maverick, *The Story of the Telegraph and a History of the Great Atlantic Cable* (New York: Rudd & Carleton, 1858), pp. 13, 22.

[6]Bob Lochte, *Christian Radio: The Growth of a Mainstream Broadcasting Force* (Jefferson, NC: McFarland & Co., 2005), p. 15.

[7]"Our Work," Christian Radio Broadcasting, accessed September 5, 2012, <www.febc.org/content/our-work>.

[8]Aimee Semple McPherson, *Bridal Call* 7 (July 1923): 15.

[9]"Pat Robertson and CBN," *Broadcasting* (March 6, 1978): 56-68.

[10]Ben Armstrong, *The Electric Church* (Nashville: Thomas Nelson, 1979), p. 171.

[11]Friedman, "The World Is Flat."

[12]Gartner Group, "Gartner's Top Predictions for IT Organizations and Users, 2010 and Beyond: A New Balance," <www.gartner.com/it/page.jsp?id =1278413>.

[13]Walt Wilson, Biola Imagination Summit 23:30–24:27, March 12, 2010.

2 Getting in the Stream

[1]Available at www.onlineschools.org/visual-academy/facebook-obsession.

[2]Alexa, the Web Information Company, "Facebook.com," <http://www .alexa.com/siteinfo/facebook.com>.

[3]Wikipedia does restrict which organizations can create entries; entries must be "notable" and "verifiable." Self-promotion is not allowed. See "Wikipedia," Wikipedia, last modified September 3, 2012, <http://en.wiki pedia.org/wiki/Wikipedia>.

[4]John Herlihy, quoted in "Google: Desktops Will Be 'Irrelevant' in Three Years," Wired, March 4, 2010, <www.wired.com/gadgetlab/2010/03/google-desktops-will-be-dead-in-three-years/>.

[5]Gartner Group, "Gartner's Top Predictions for IT Organizations and Users, 2010 and Beyond: A New Balance."

[6]Mary Meeker, "Internet Trends" (the Web 2.0 summit in San Francisco, Calif., October 18, 2011). Meek's data were taken from a variety of sources; for more detail, see her presentation notes at <http://kpcb.com/ insights/2011-internet-trends>.

[7]B. J. Fogg, "The Future of Persuasion is Mobile," in Mobile Persuasion: 20 Perspectives of the Future of Behavior Change, ed. B. J. Fogg and Dean Eckles (Stanford, CA: Stanford Captology Media, 2007), p. 6.

[8]Mirjana Spasojevic, Rachel Hinman and Will Dzierson, "Mobile Persua-sion Design Principles," in Mobile Persuasion: 20 Perspectives of the Future of Behavior Change, ed. B. J. Fogg and Dean Eckles (Stanford, CA: Stanford Captology Media, 2007), pp. 119-20.

[9]See Table 2.2.

3 Creating Change

[1]Walt Wilson, interview with the author, April 13, 2010.

[2]Ibid.

[3]U.S. stats from "Internet Users in North America March 31, 2011," Internet World Stats, accessed October 12, 2012, <www.internetworldstats.com/ stats14.htm>. World stats from "Internet Users in the World, Internet World Stats, accessed October 12, 2012, <www.internetworldstats.com/ stats.htm>.

[4]Data in these figures come from Pew Internet & American Life Project Tracking surveys (March 2000–February 2012). Please note that the word-ing for some items has been abbreviated. For full question wording, please refer to the questionnaire available at <www.pewinternet.org/Trend-Data-

(Adults)/usage-over-time.aspx>.

[5]Aubrey Malphurs and Michael Malphurs, *Church Next: Using the Internet to Maximize Your Ministry* (Grand Rapids: Kregel Publications, 2003).

[6]Ibid., p. 61.

[7]Ibid., p. 62.

[8]See Aubrey Malphurs, *Advanced Strategic Planning: A New Model for Church and Ministry Leaders,* 2nd ed. (Grand Rapids: Baker Books, 2005), and Peter Drucker, *Managing the Nonprofit Organization: Principles and Practices,* reprint ed. (New York: HarperBusiness, 2006).

[9]Malphurs and Malphurs, *Church Next,* p. 67.

[10]Ibid., p. 70.

[11]Ibid., p. 73.

[12]Marshall McLuhan, *Understanding Media* (New York: McGraw-Hill, 1964), p. 32.

[13]Shane Hipps, *The Hidden Power of Electronic Culture: How Media Shapes Faith, the Gospel, and the Church* (Grand Rapids: Zondervan, 2005), p. 58.

[14]Shane Hipps, interview with the author, January 28, 2009.

[15]Walt Wilson, interview with the author, April 13, 2010.

4 The Digital Ministry Framework

[1]"Success," for the purposes of this survey, was defined by a series of questions regarding how participants viewed their website.

5 Planning Your Digital Strategy

[1]Edward R. Dayton and David Allen Fraser, *Planning Strategies for World Evangelization,* rev. ed. (Grand Rapids: Eerdmans, 1990), p. 14.

[2]Viggo Søgaard, *Media in Church and Mission: Communicating the Gospel* (Pasadena: William Carey Library, 1993), pp. 56-57.

7 Privacy and Security Considerations for Digital Ministry

[1]"2012 Consumer Privacy Index," TRUSTe, accessed September 5, 2012, <www.truste.com/consumer-privacy-index-Q1-2012/>.

[2]Mary Madden, "Privacy Management on Social Media Sites," Pew Internet & American Life Project, February 24, 2012, <www.pewinternet.org/Reports/2012/Privacy-management-on-social-media.aspx>.

About the Author

David T. Bourgeois (PhD, Claremont Graduate University), is director of innovation and associate professor of information systems at Crowell School of Business at Biola University. He has worked in information systems at Fortune 500 companies in such roles as systems analyst, programmer, project leader, trainer and consultant. Dave has been researching and consulting on the use of digital technologies by churches, ministries and other faith-based institutions for the past several years. Dave has a passion to help these organizations use digital tools to more effectively love God and love others. He can be found online at ministryinthedigitalage .com and on Twitter at: twitter.com/DaveBourgeois.